Black and White Portfolio 2017

Author/Photographer/Publisher
Ian McKenzie

ISBN-13: 978-1543145038
ISBN-10: 1543145035

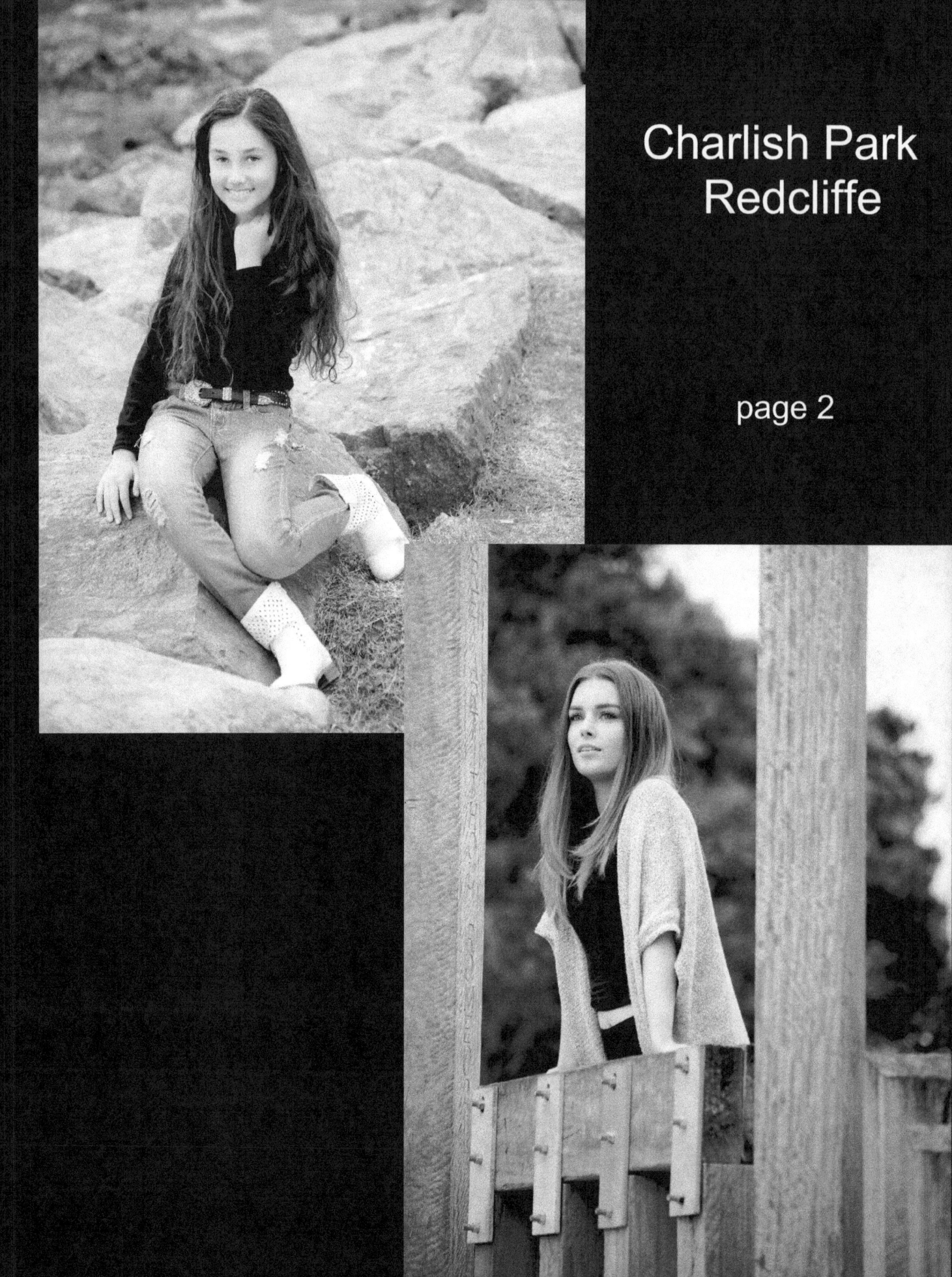

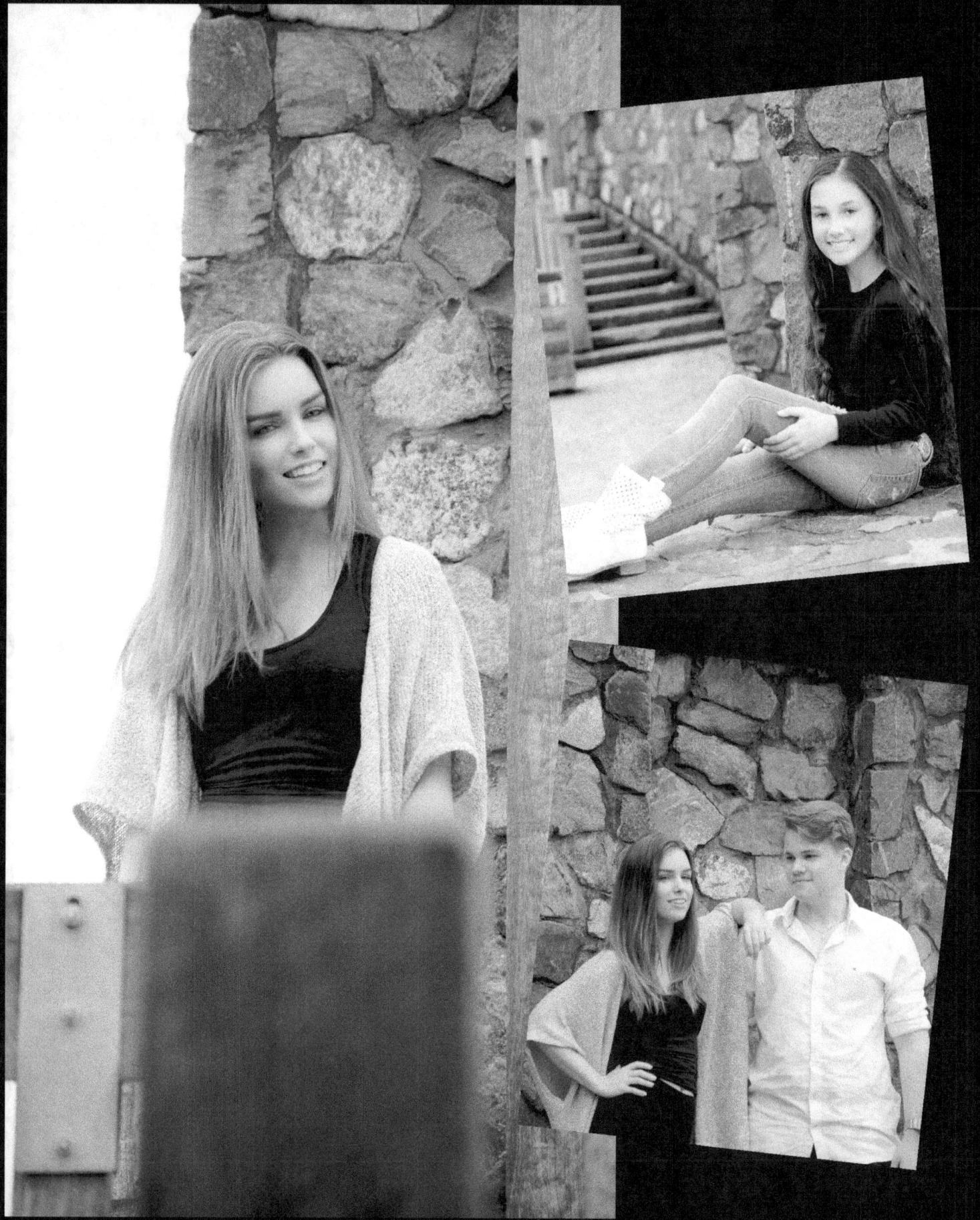

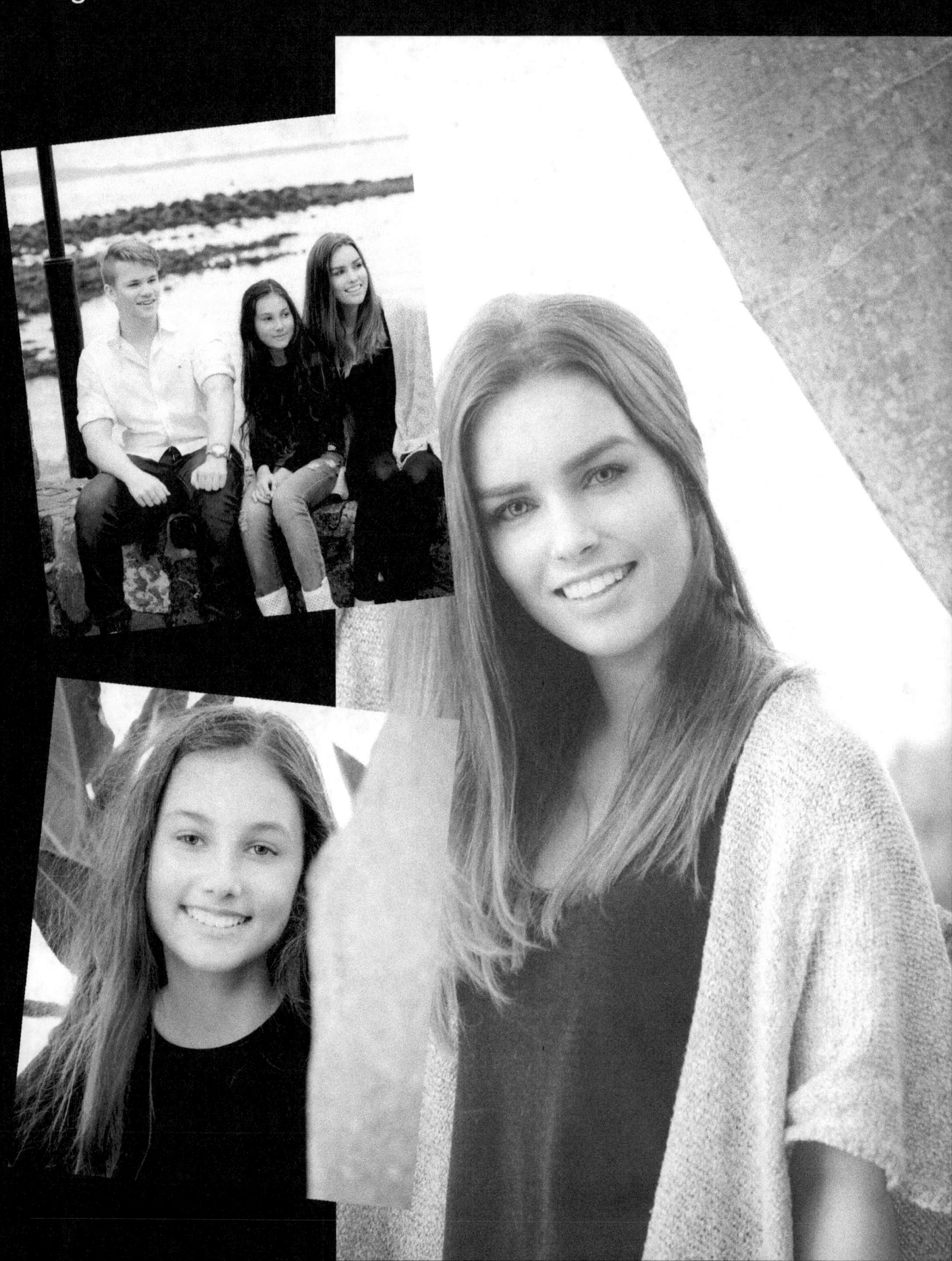

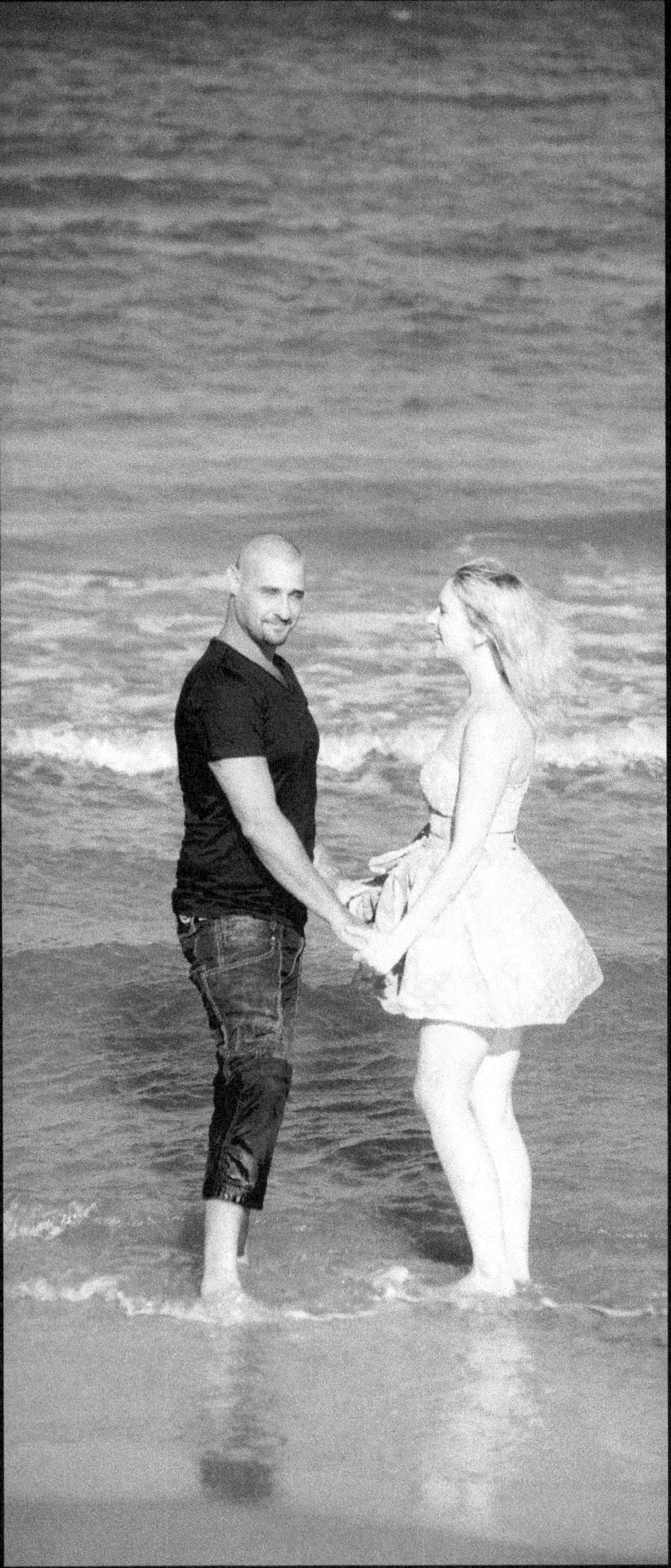

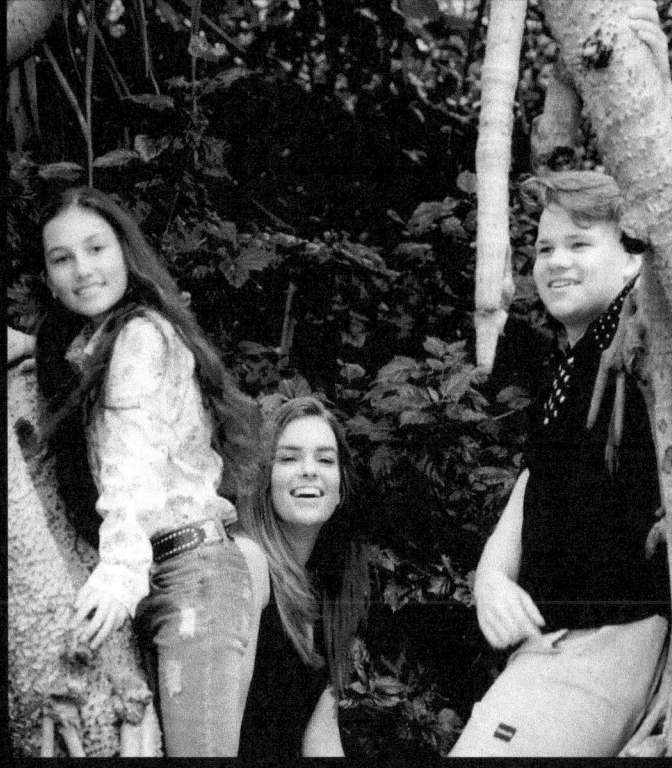

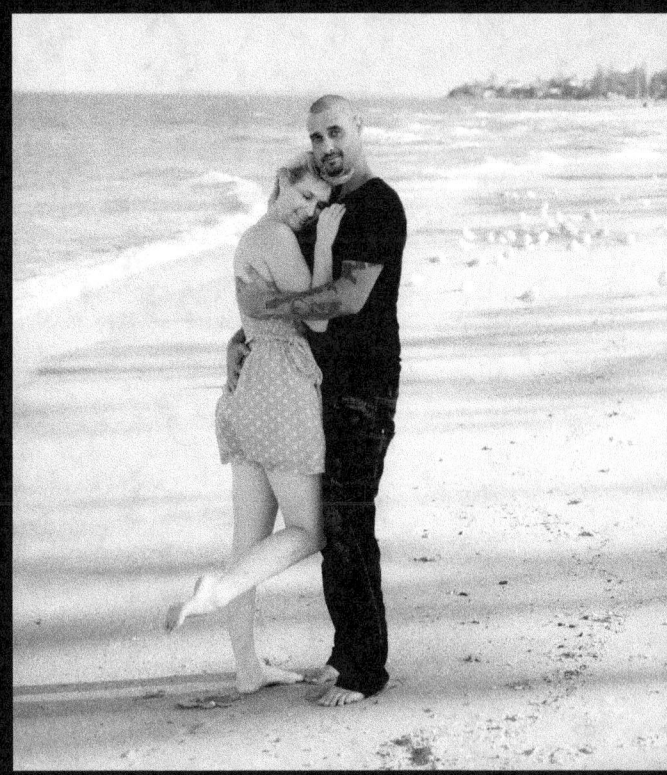

Suttons Beach Redcliffe

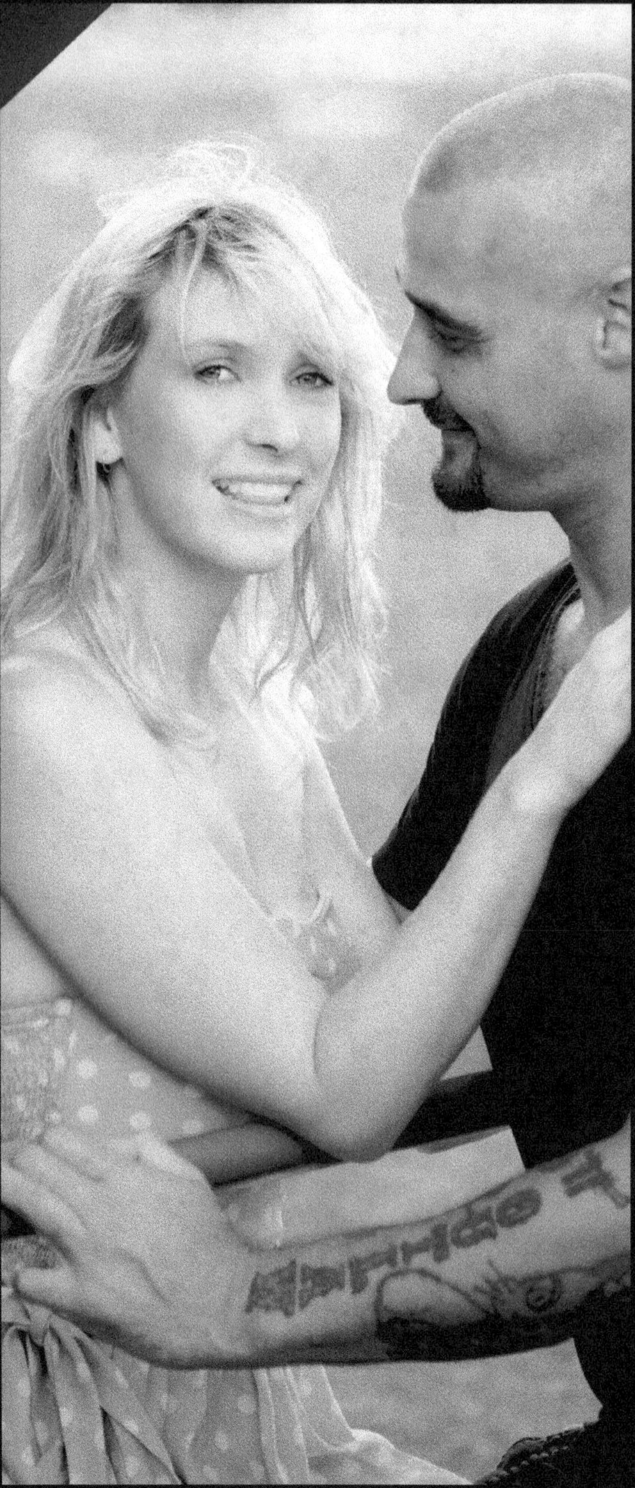

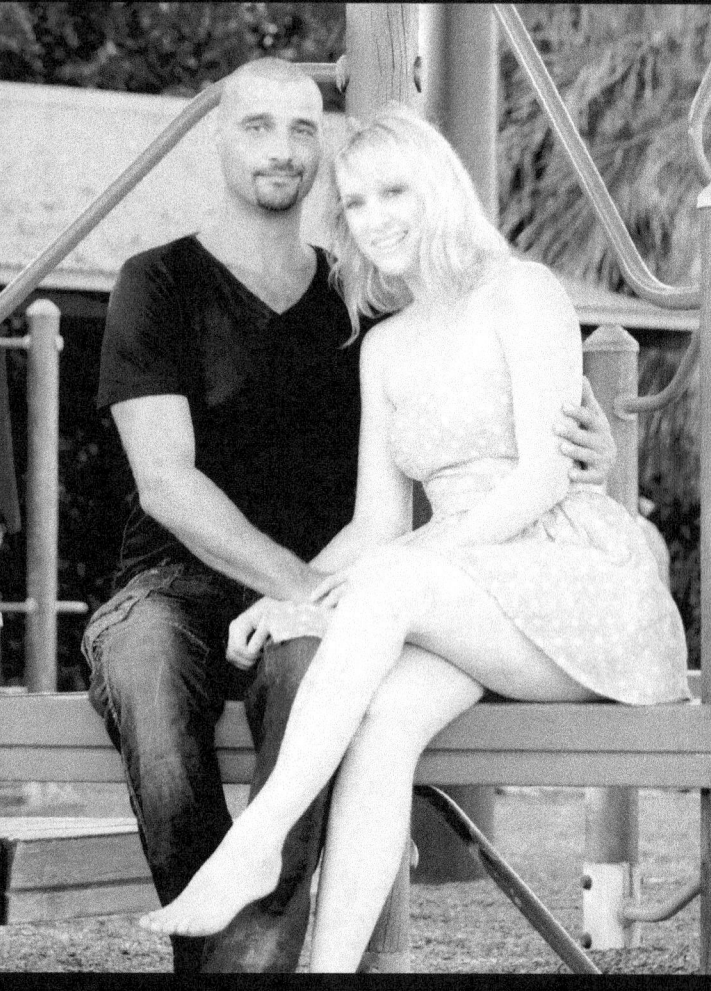
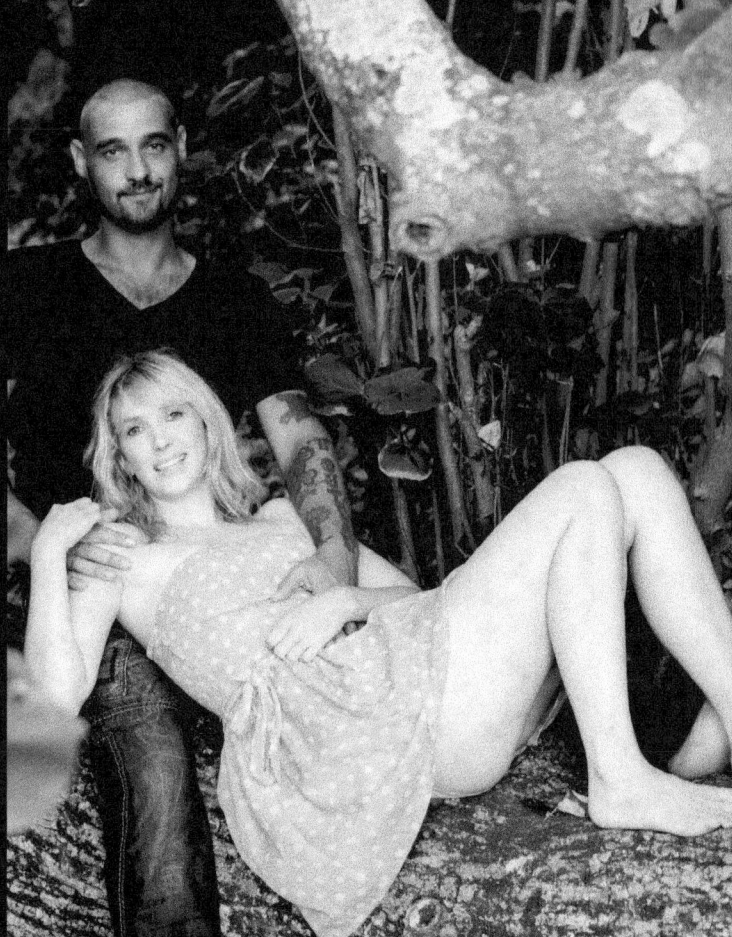

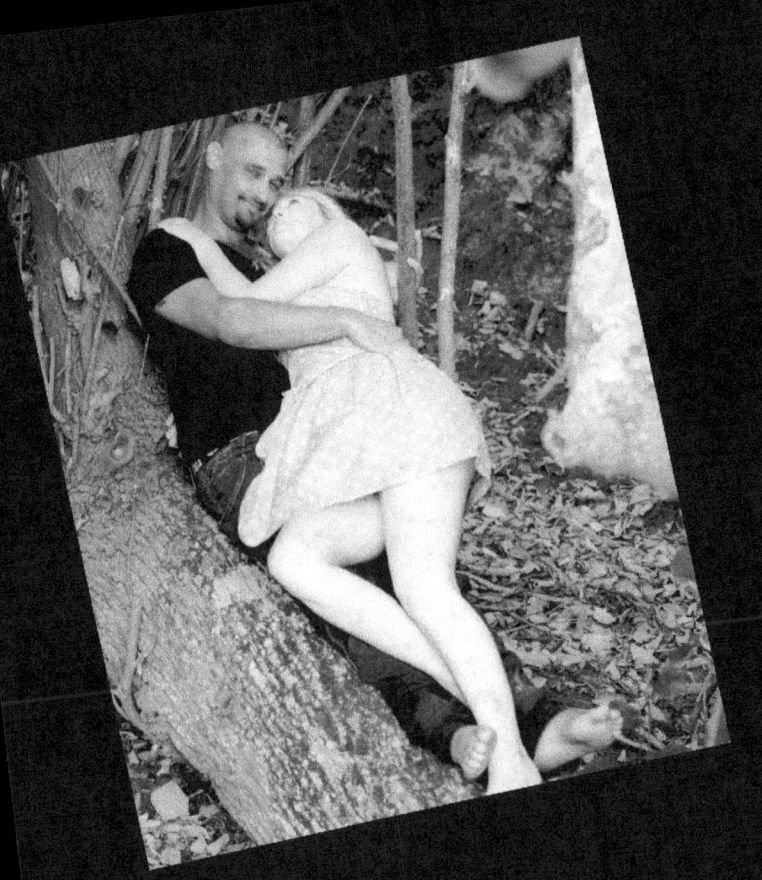

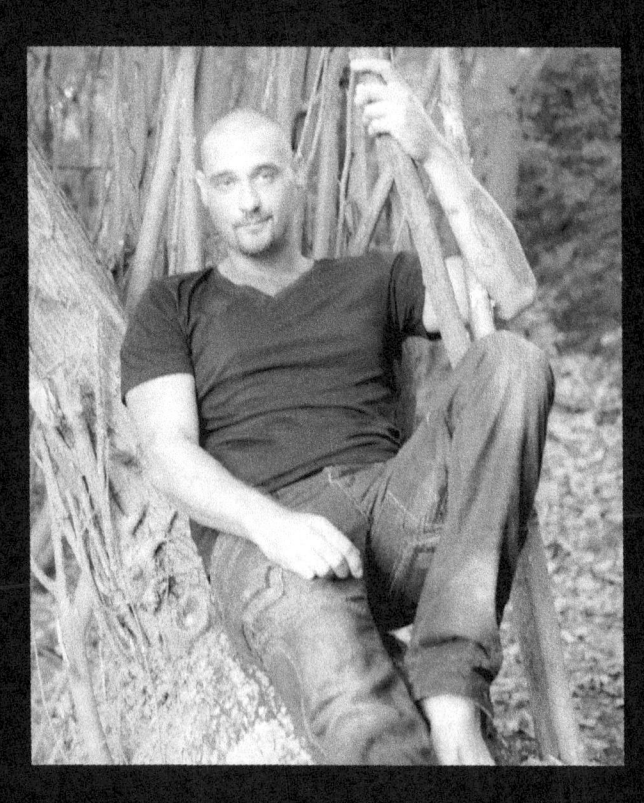

Photos above taken at Redcliffe - Photos below taken at Benowa on the Gold Coast

page 7

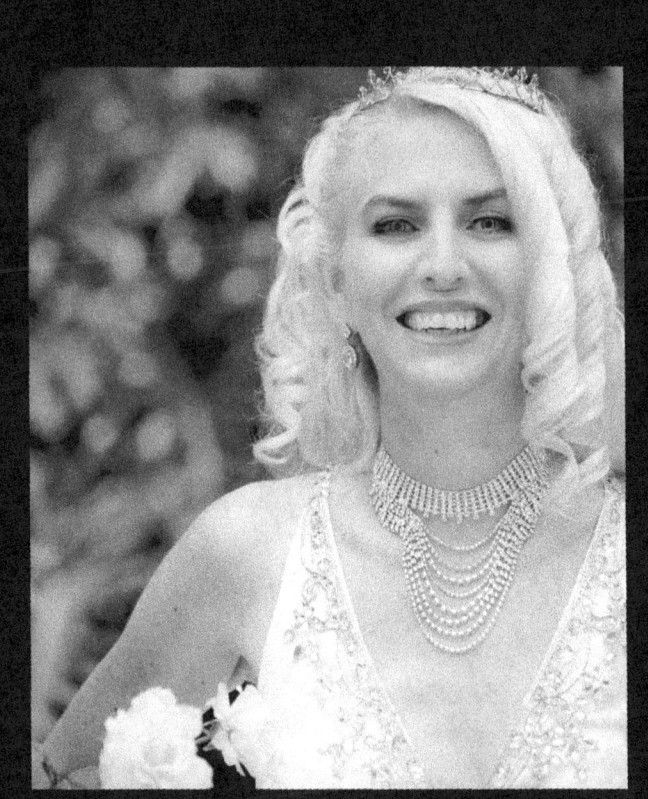

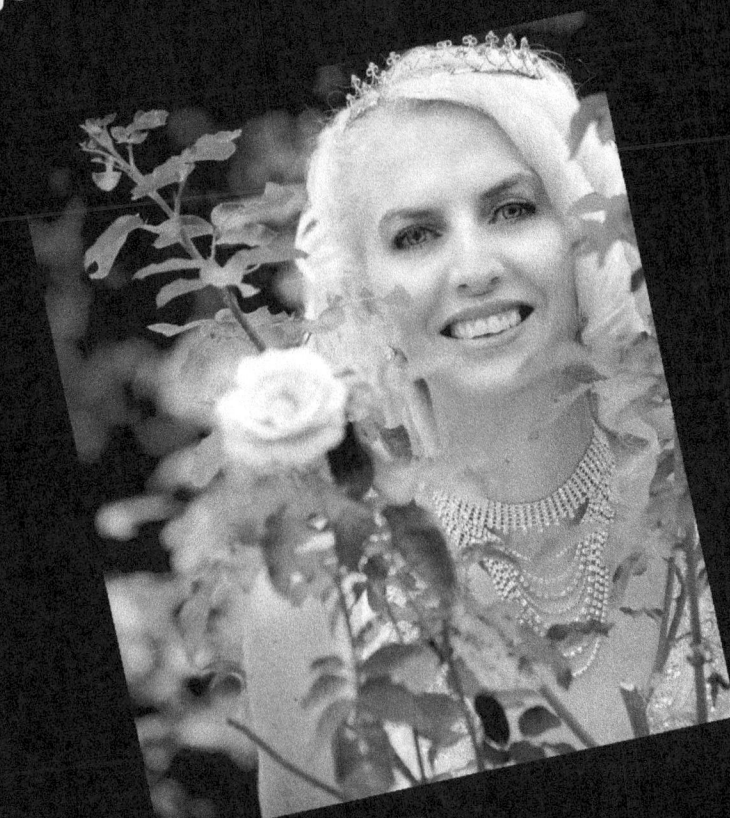

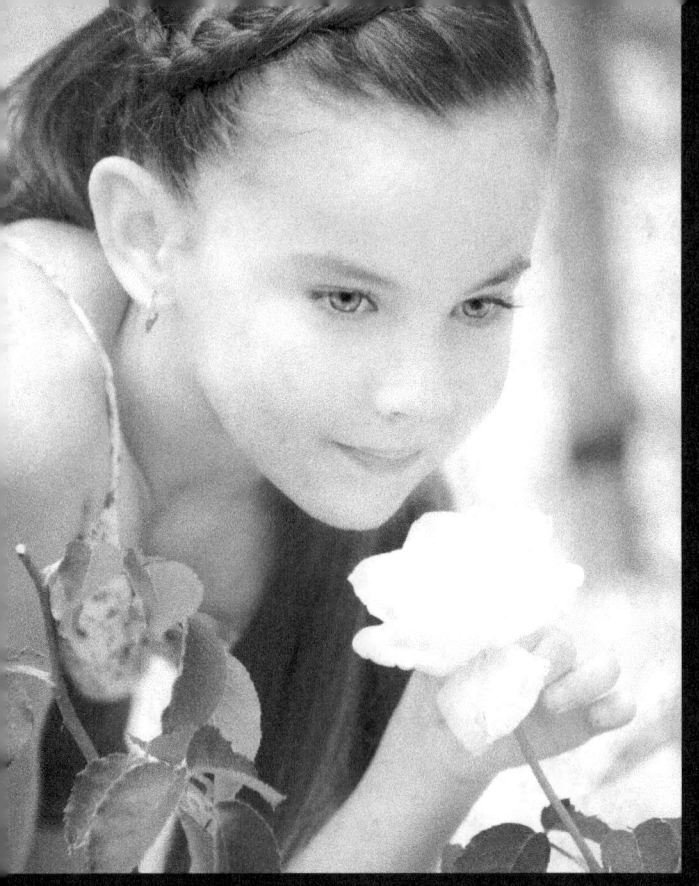
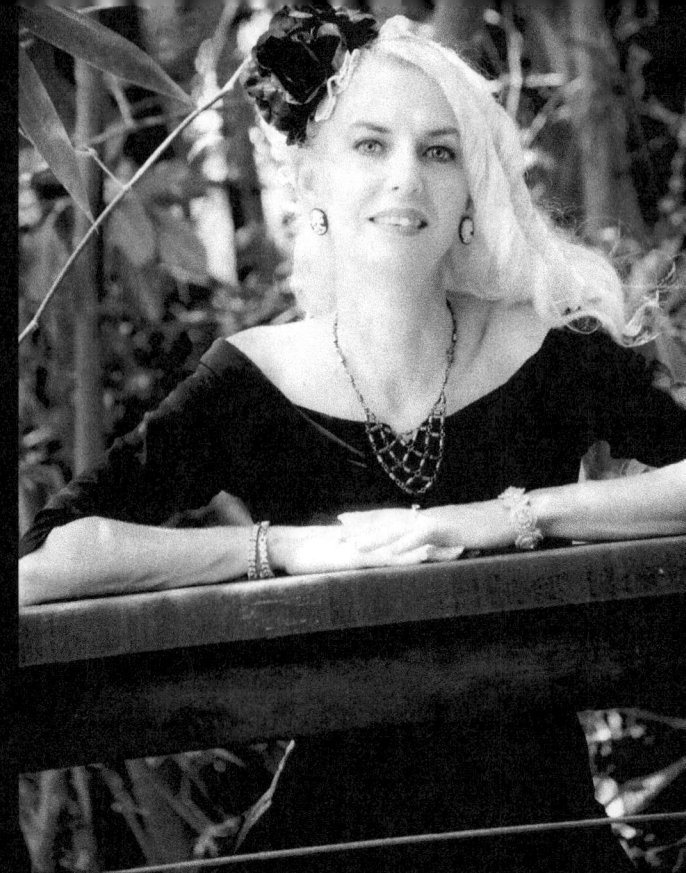

Photos above Benowa - Photos below Calamvale
page 8

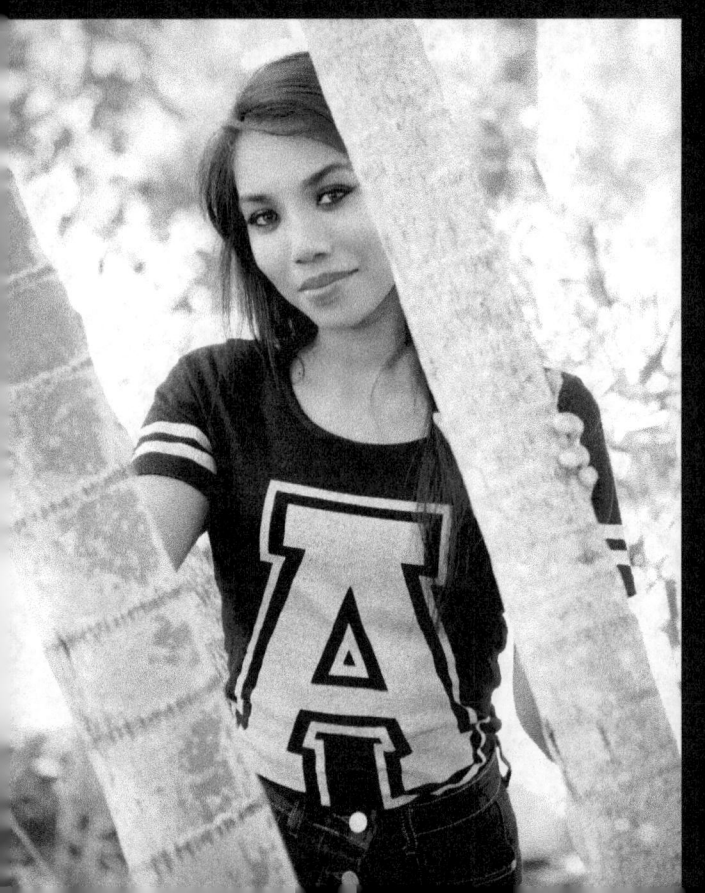
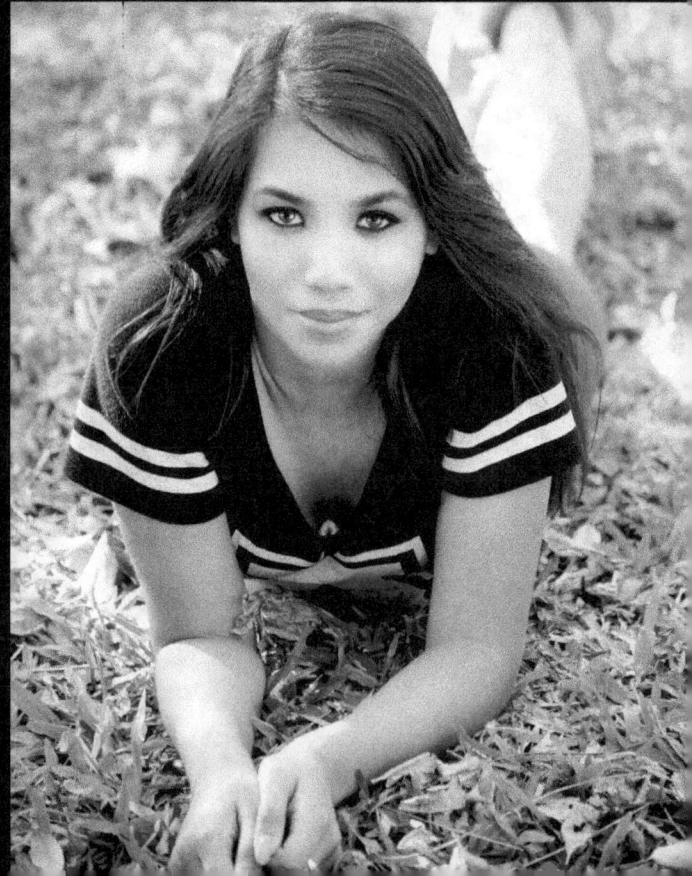

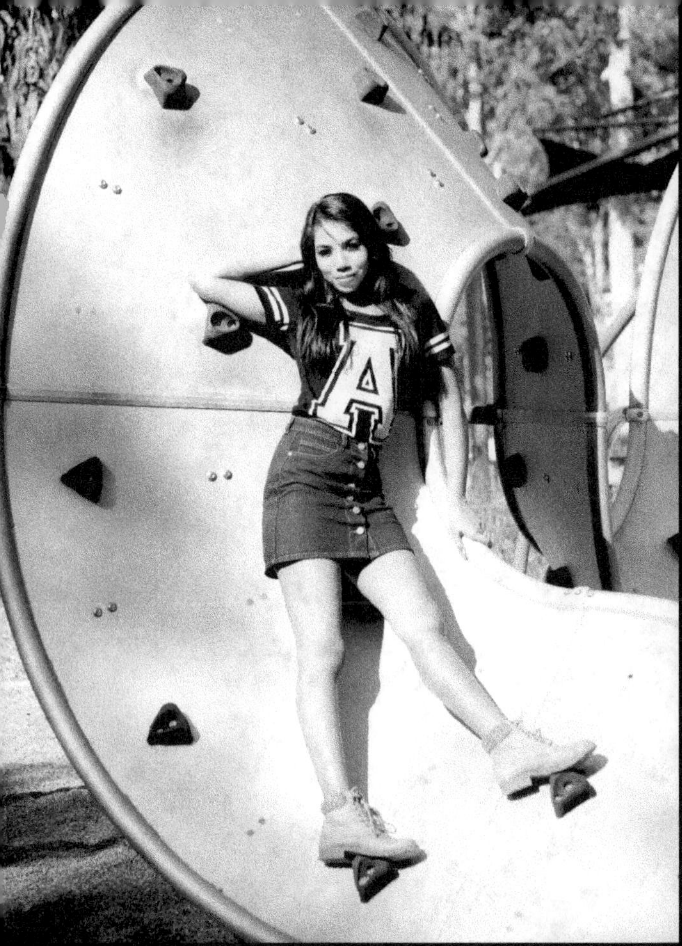

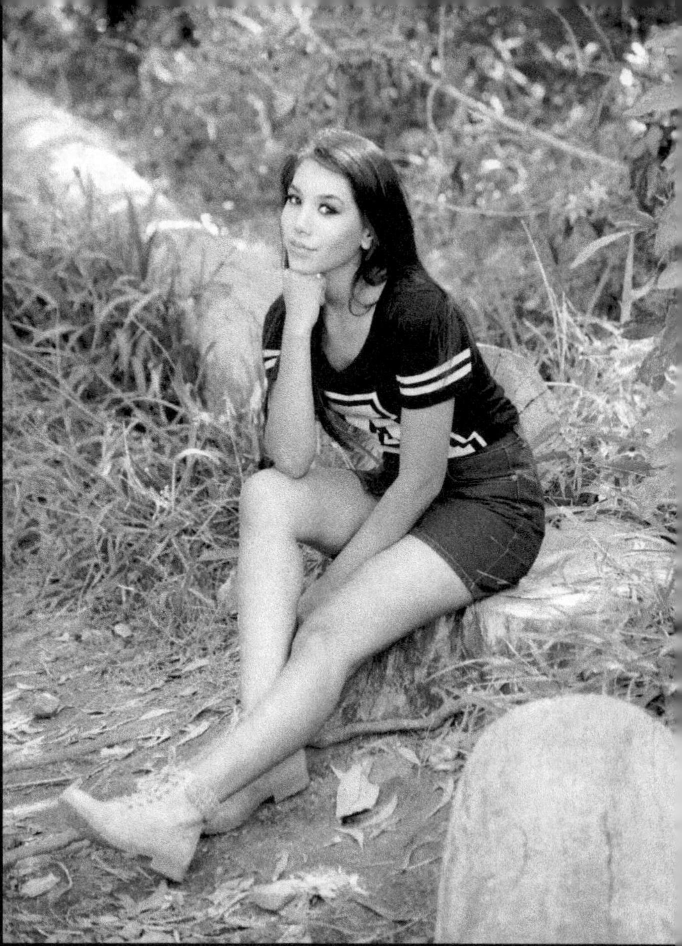

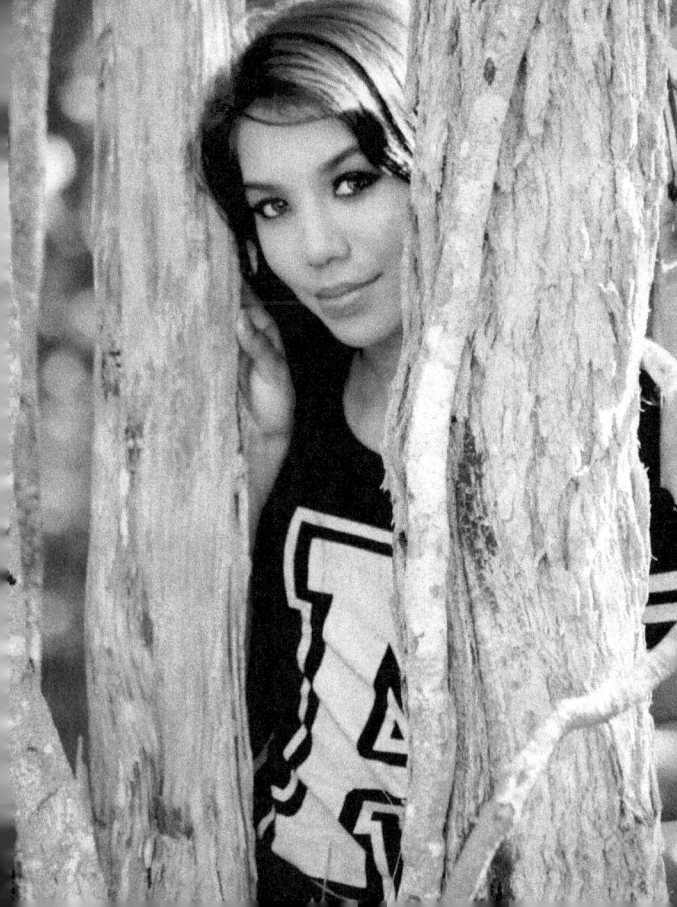
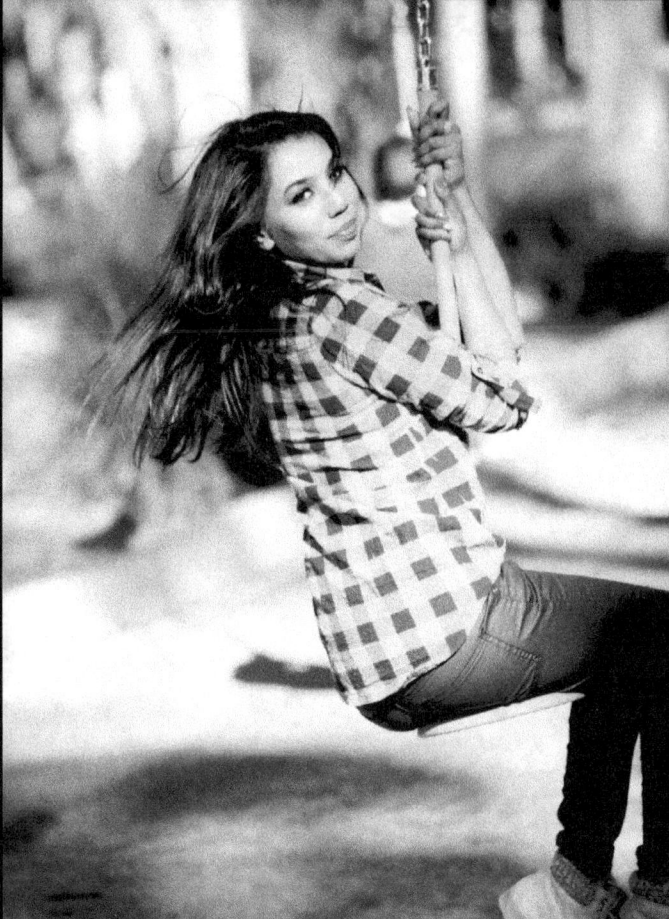

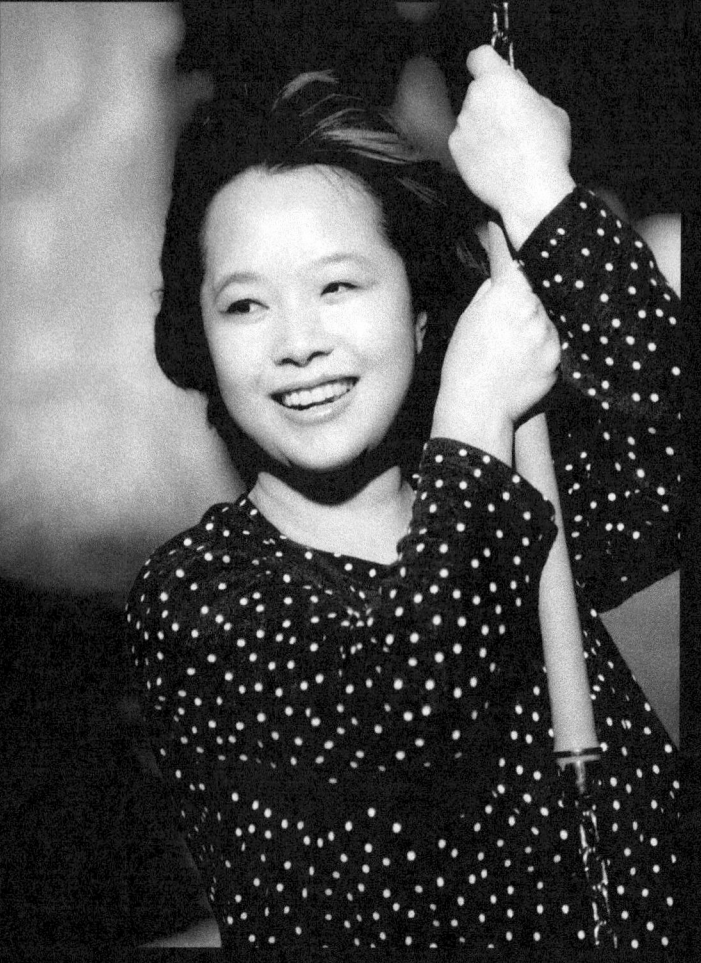
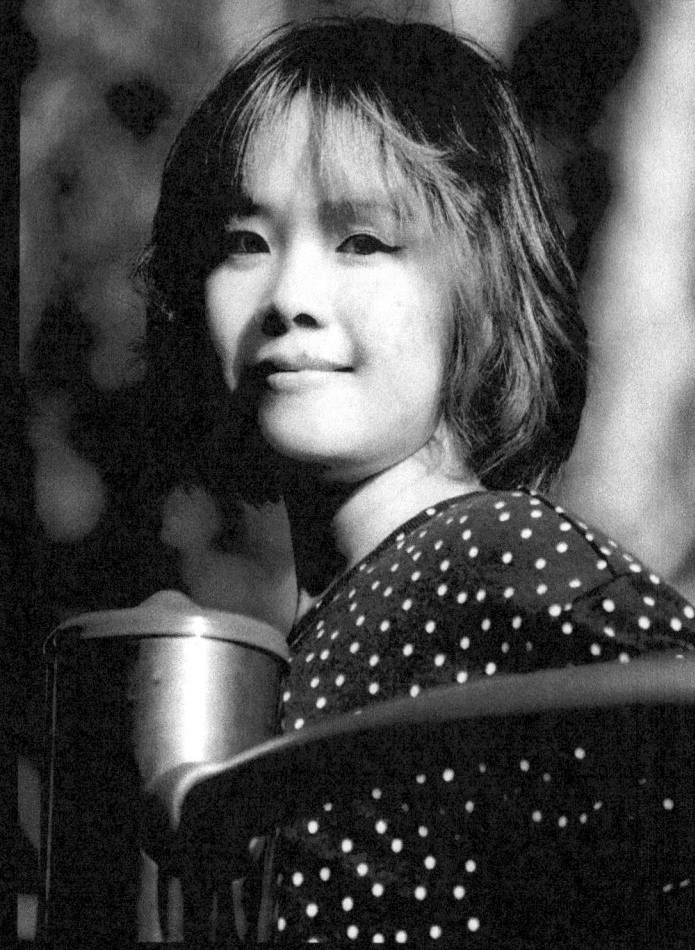
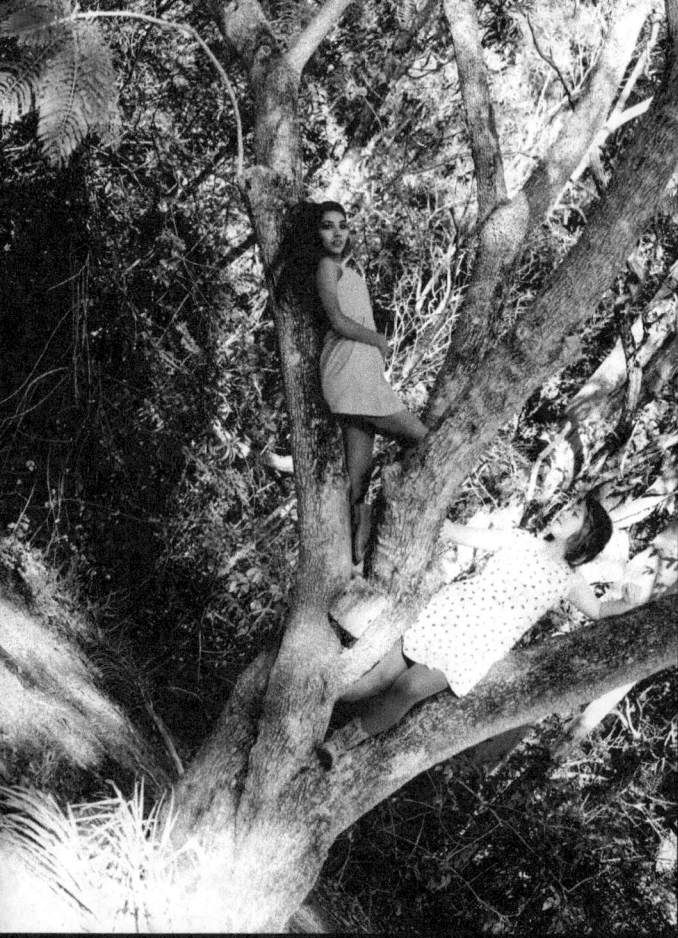

Calamvale District Park

page 10

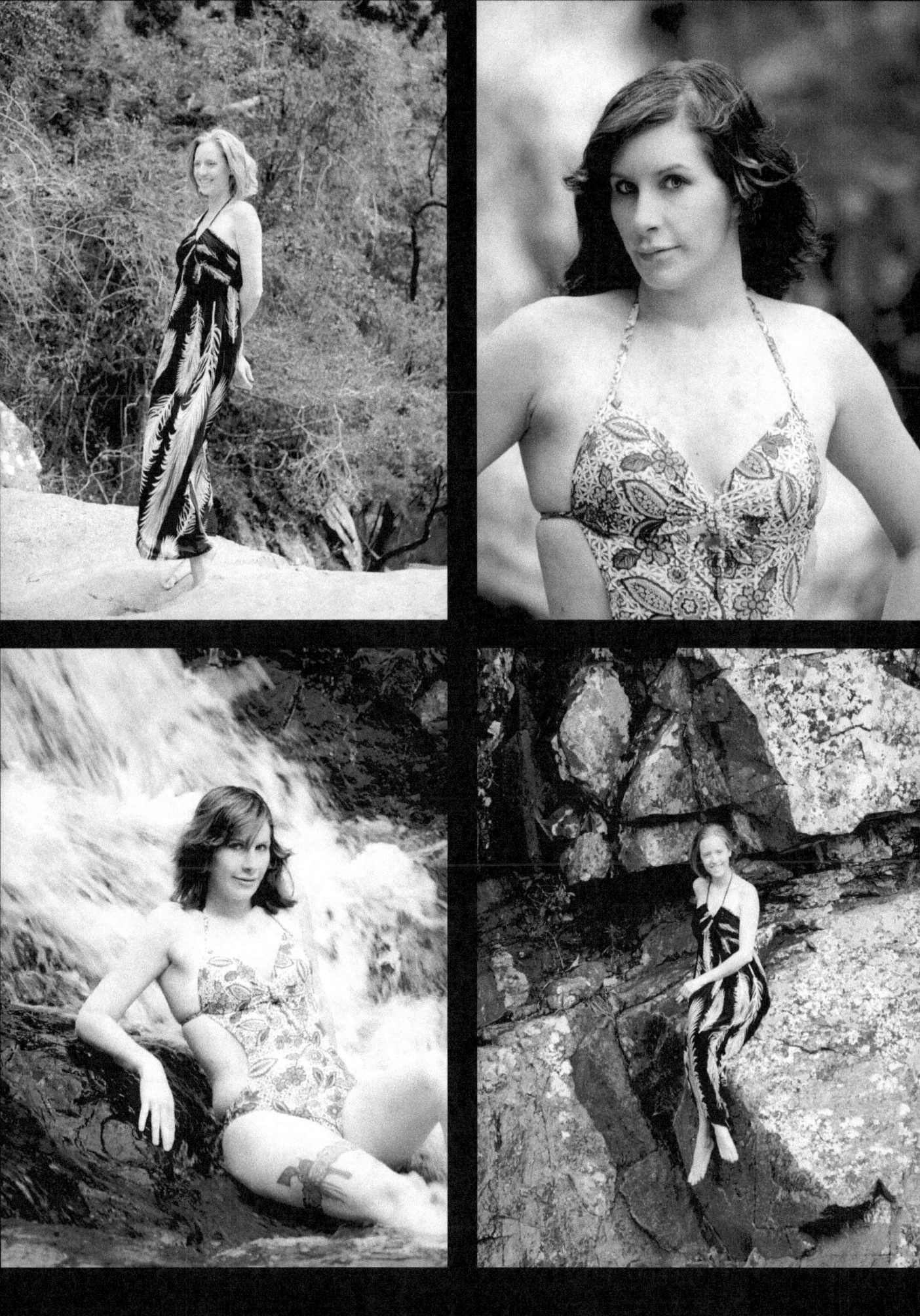

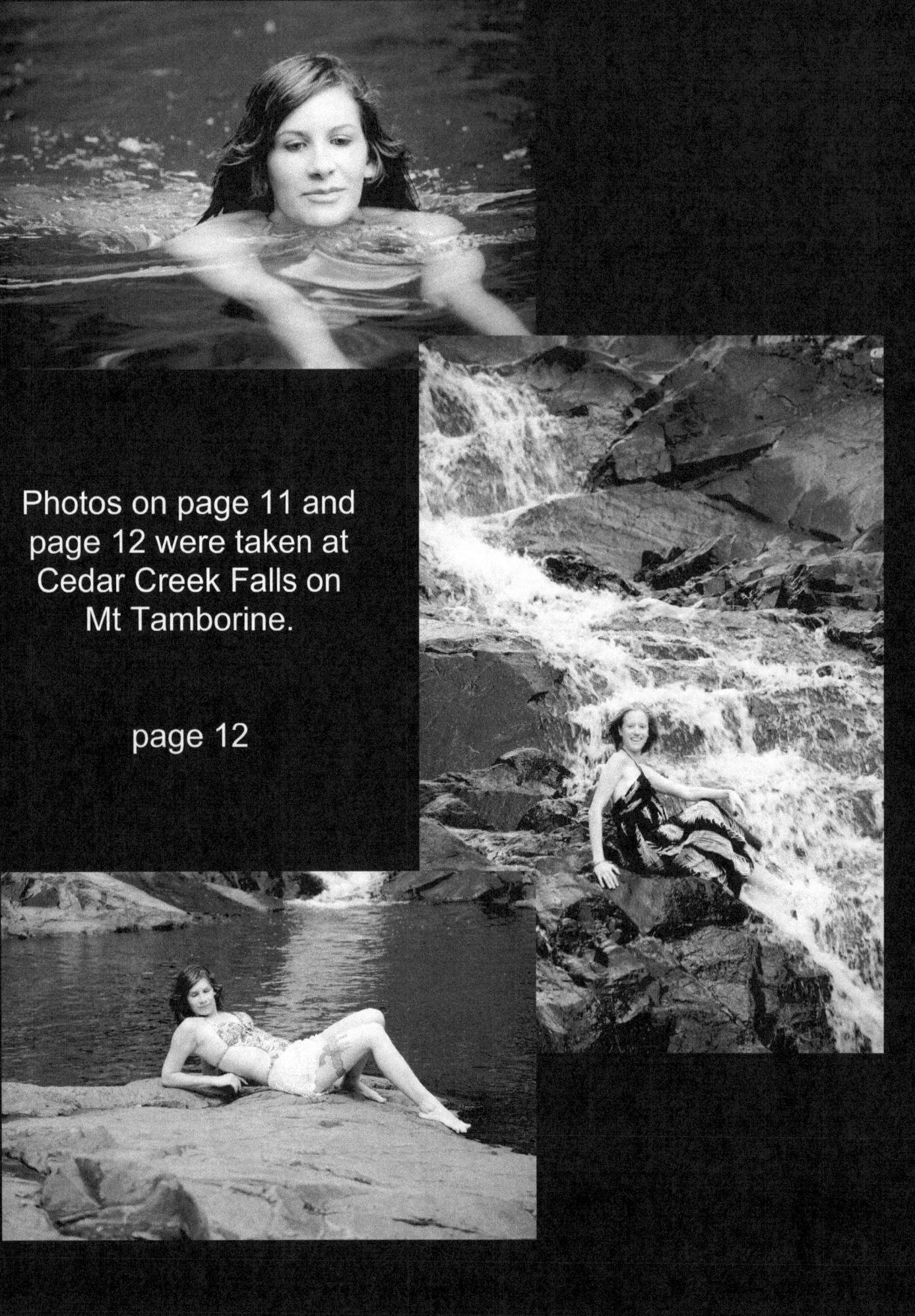

Photos on page 11 and
page 12 were taken at
Cedar Creek Falls on
Mt Tamborine.

page 12

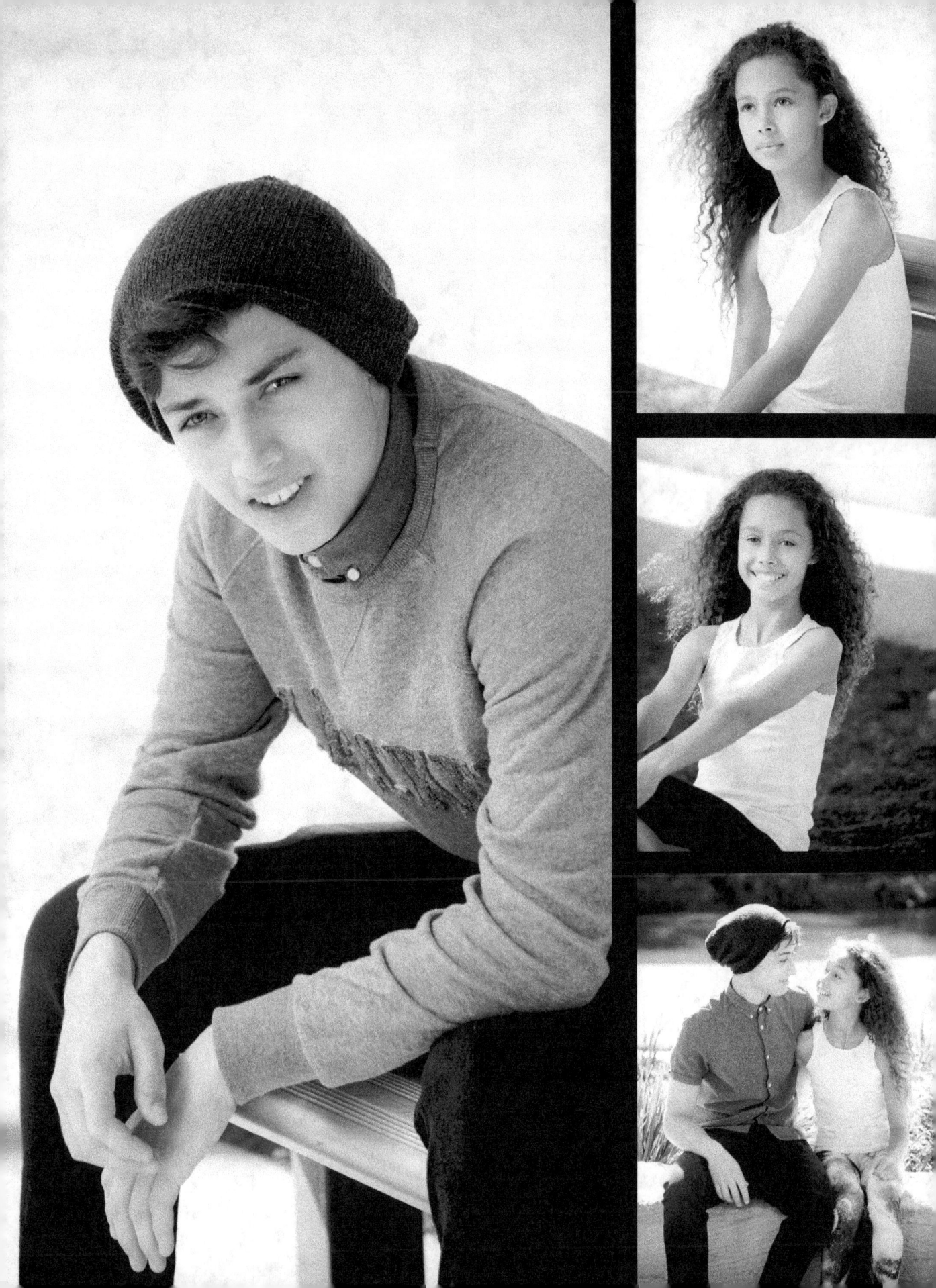

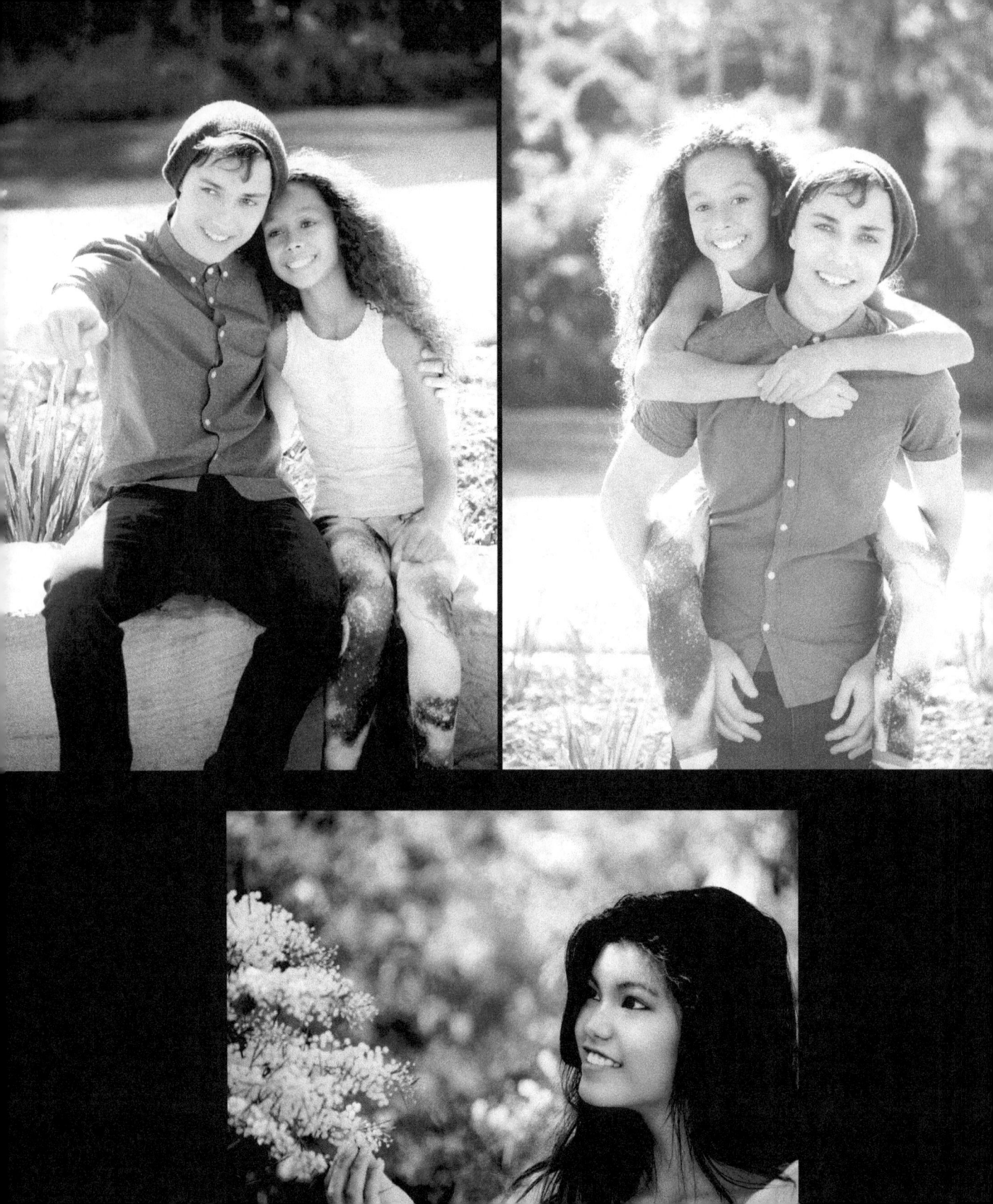

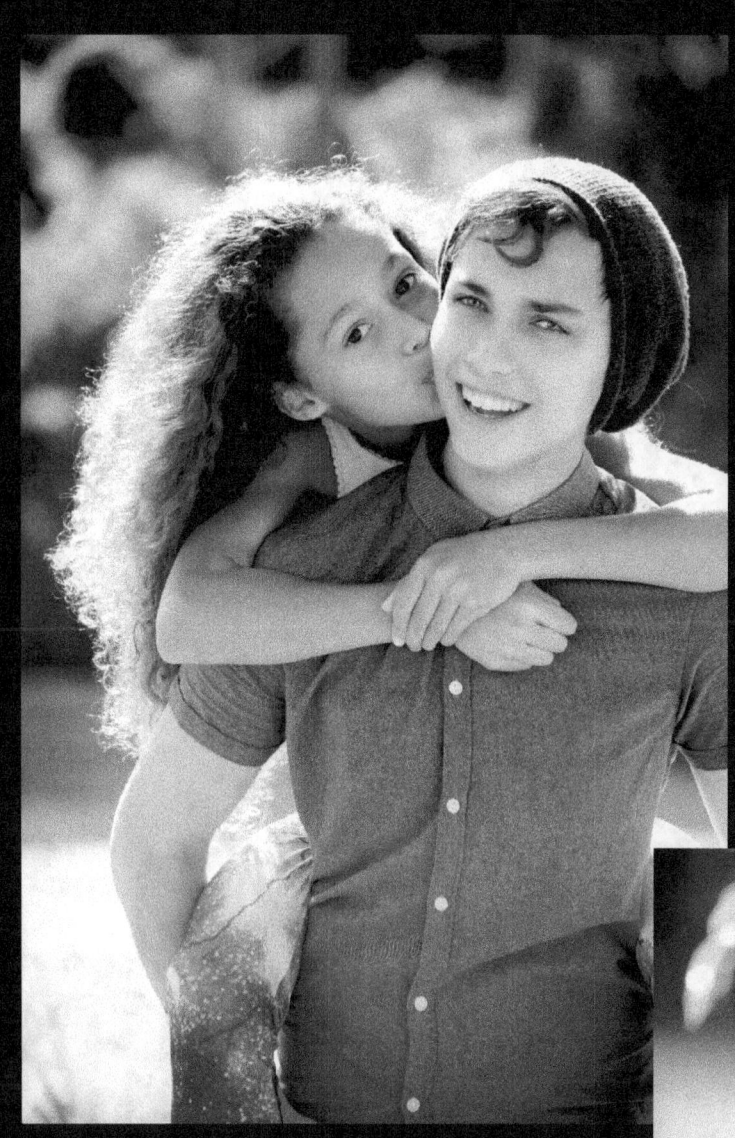

Photos on pages 13, 14 and 15 were taken at Colleges Crossing

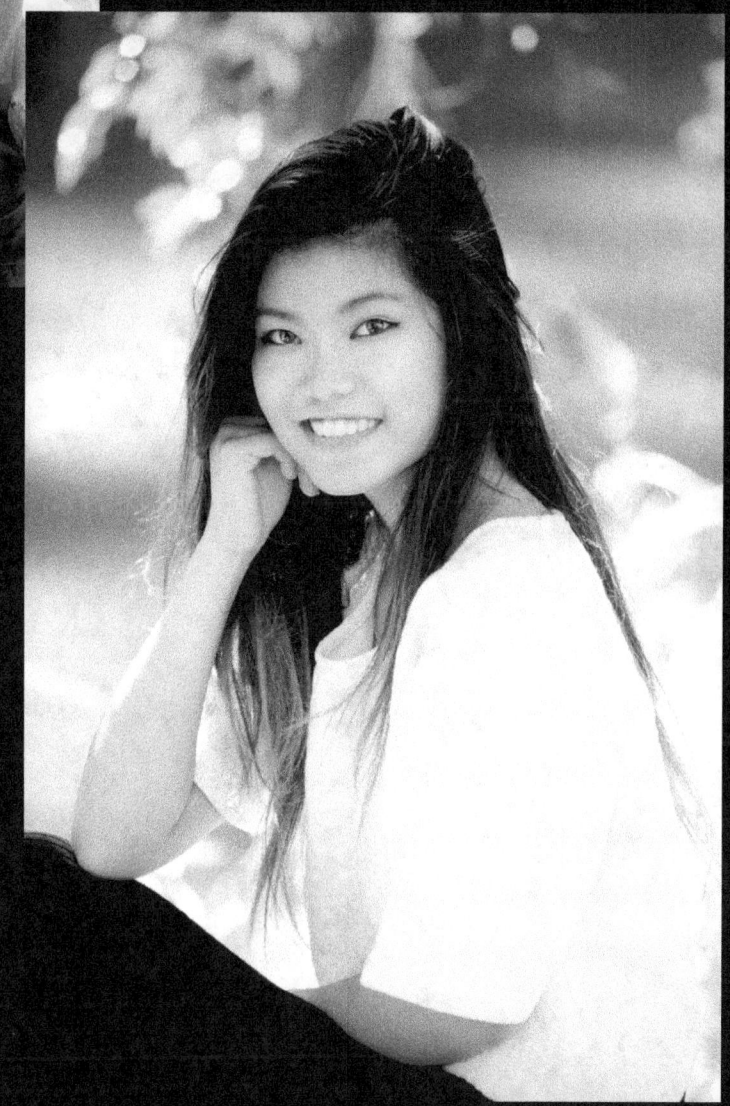

page 15

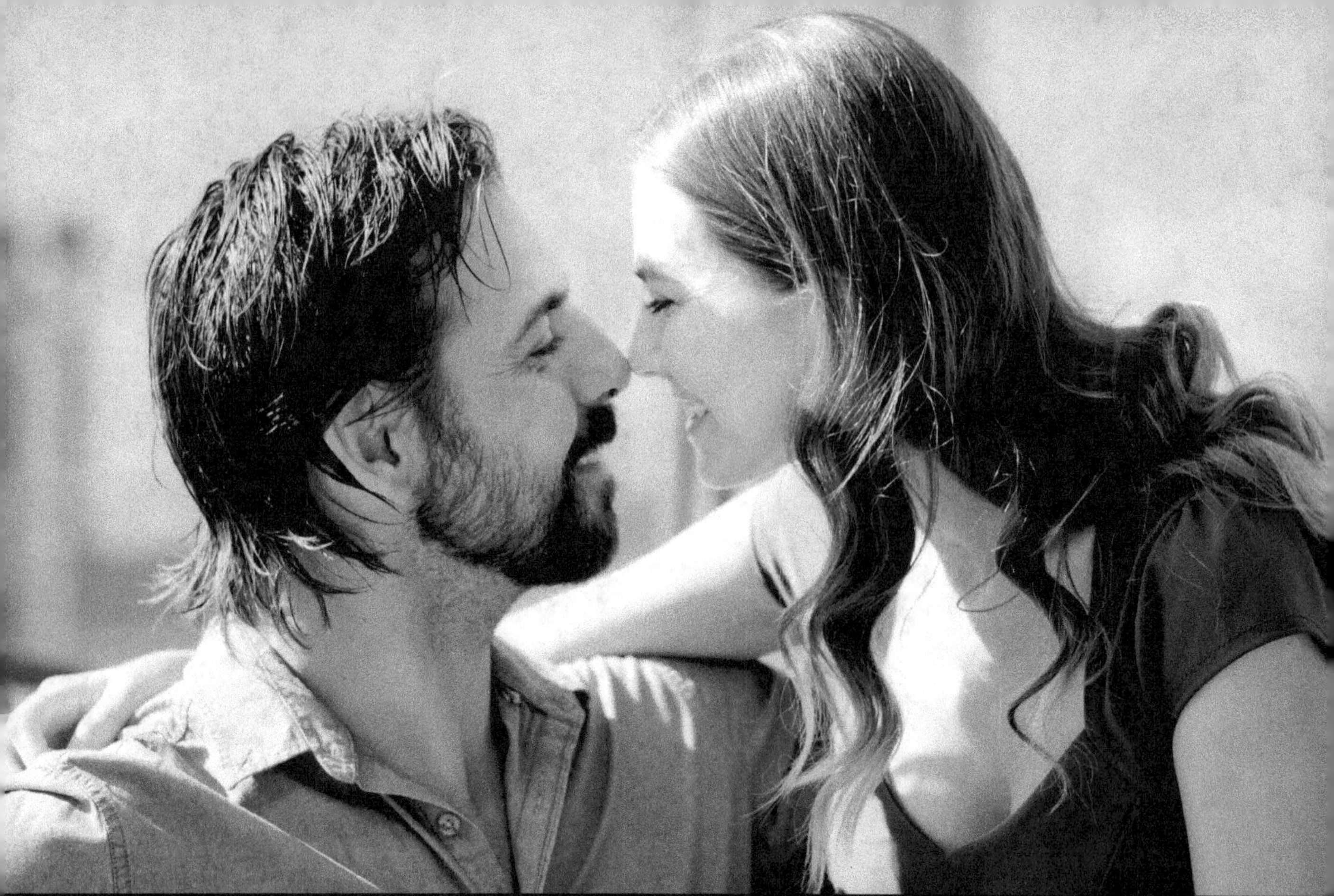

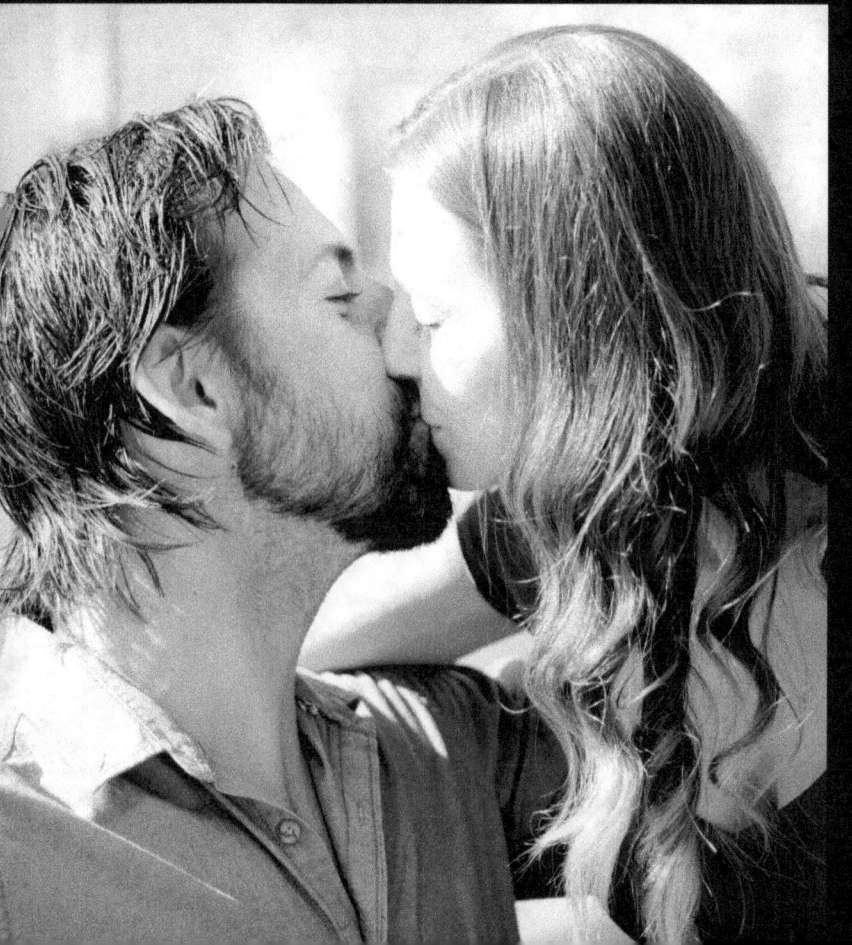

Valentines Day
couples shoot at
Brisbane Riverside

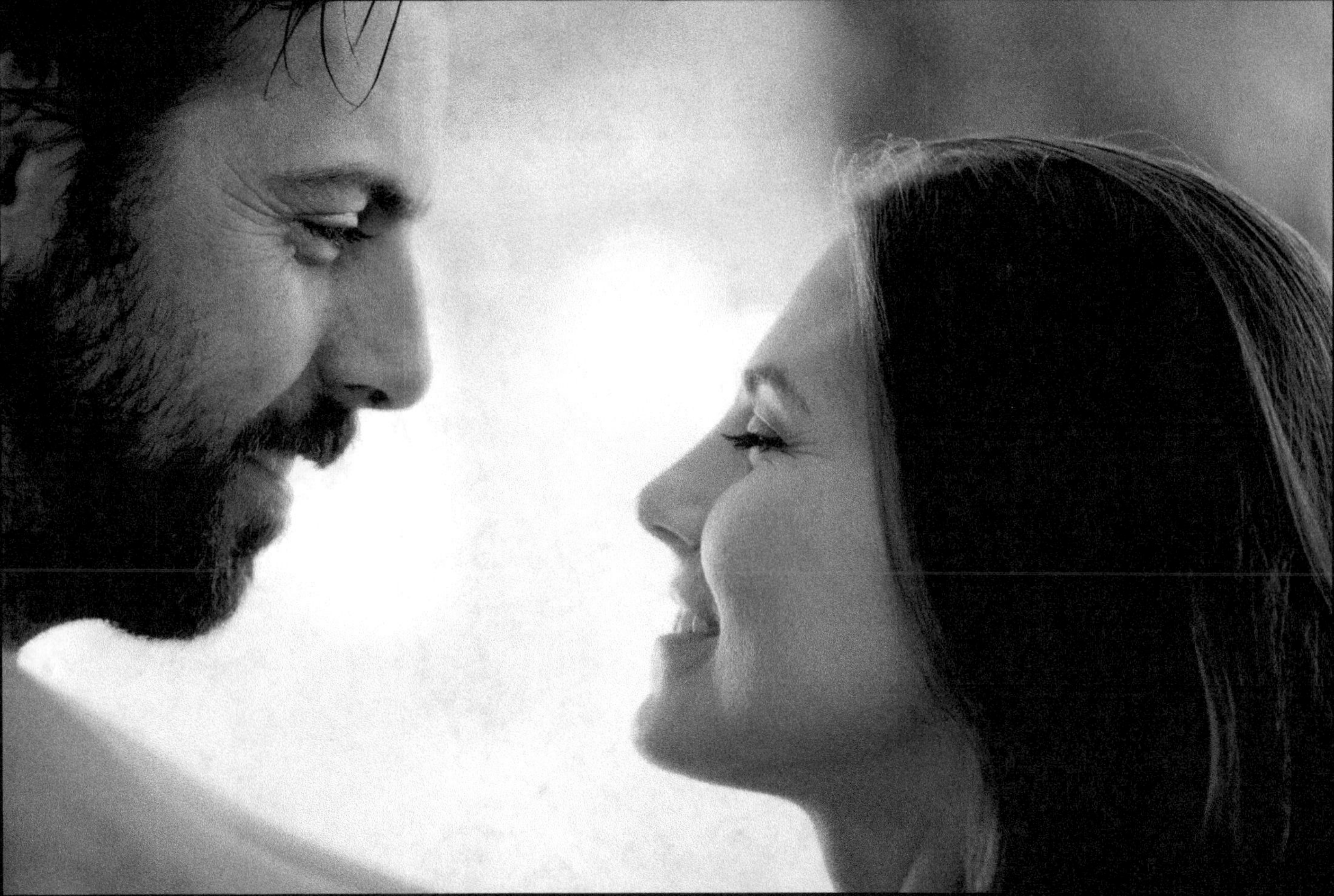

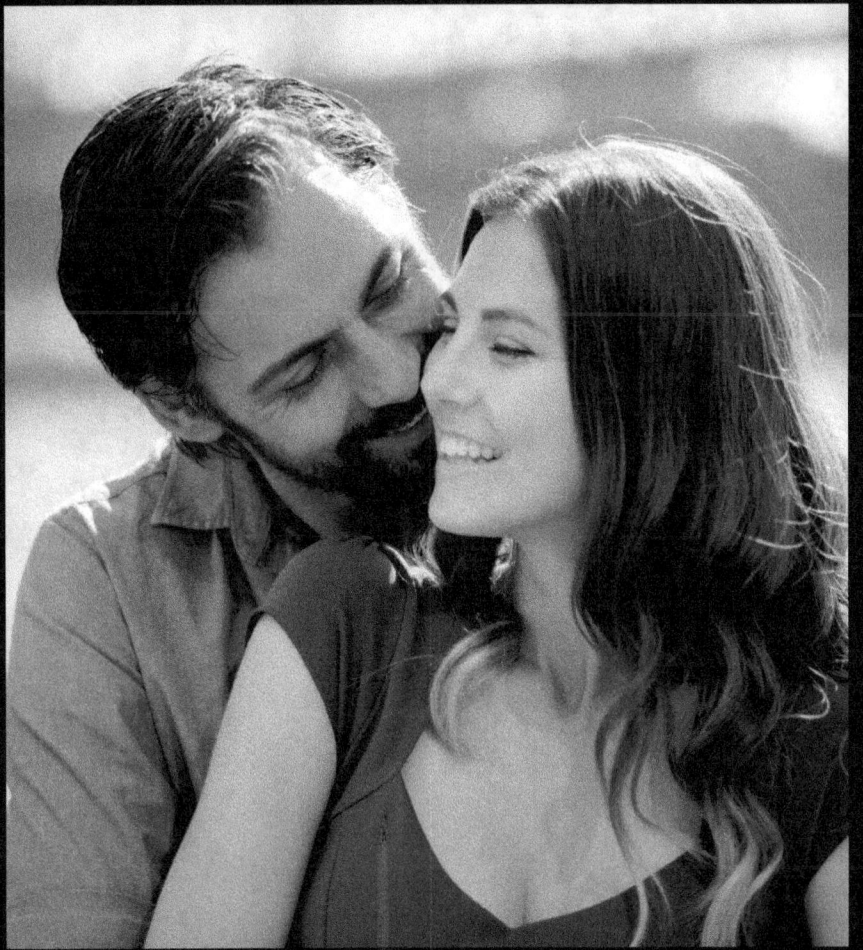

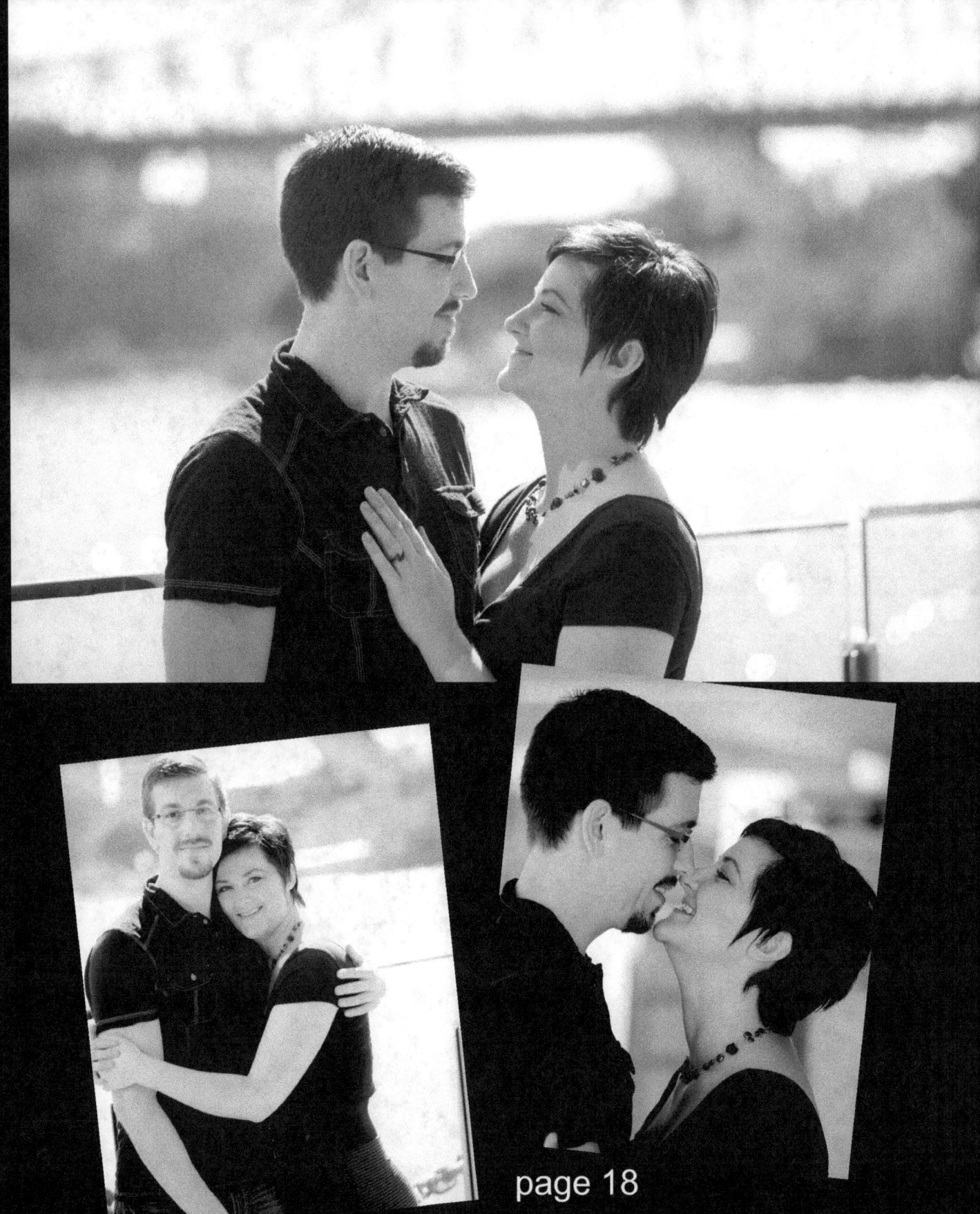

page 18

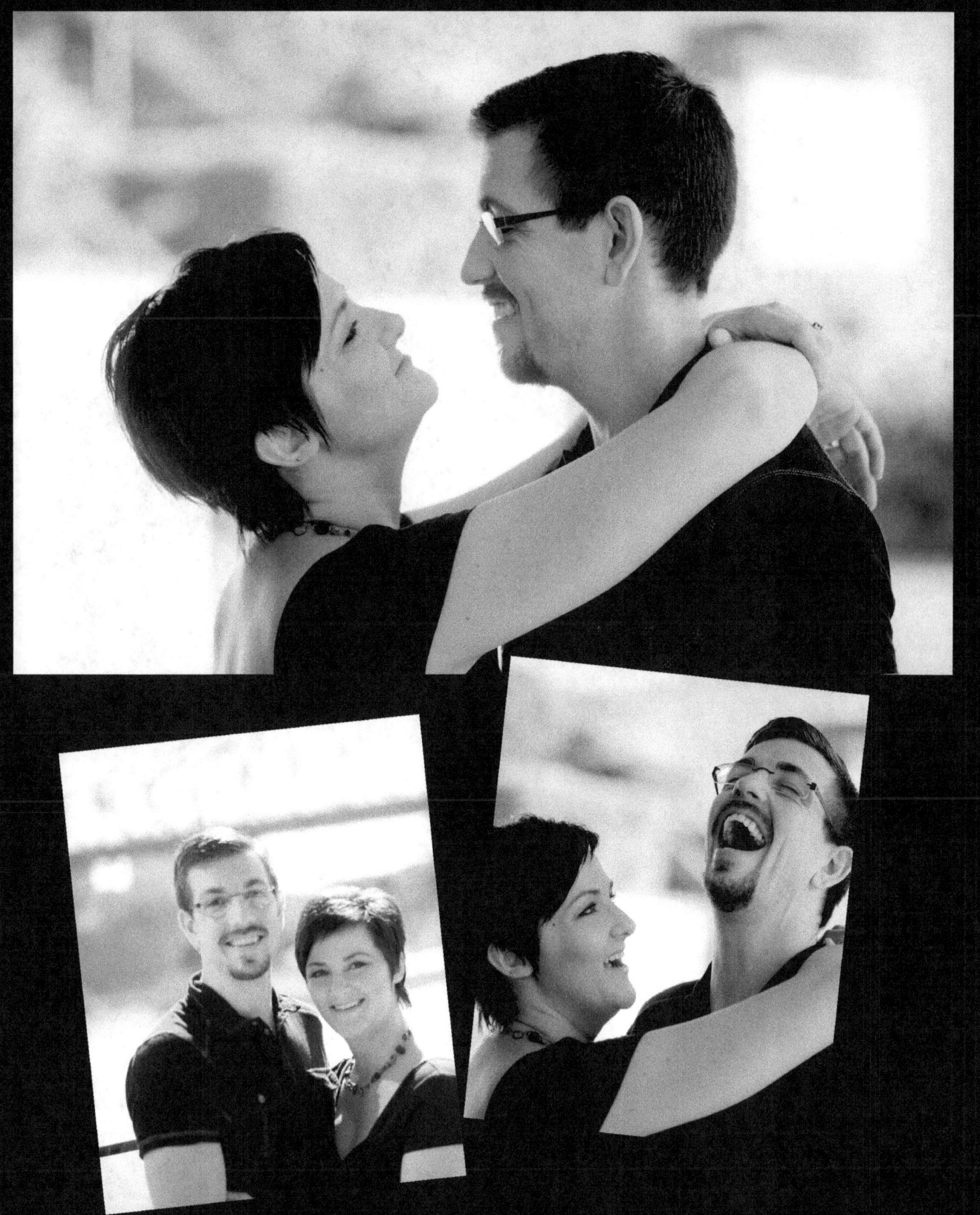

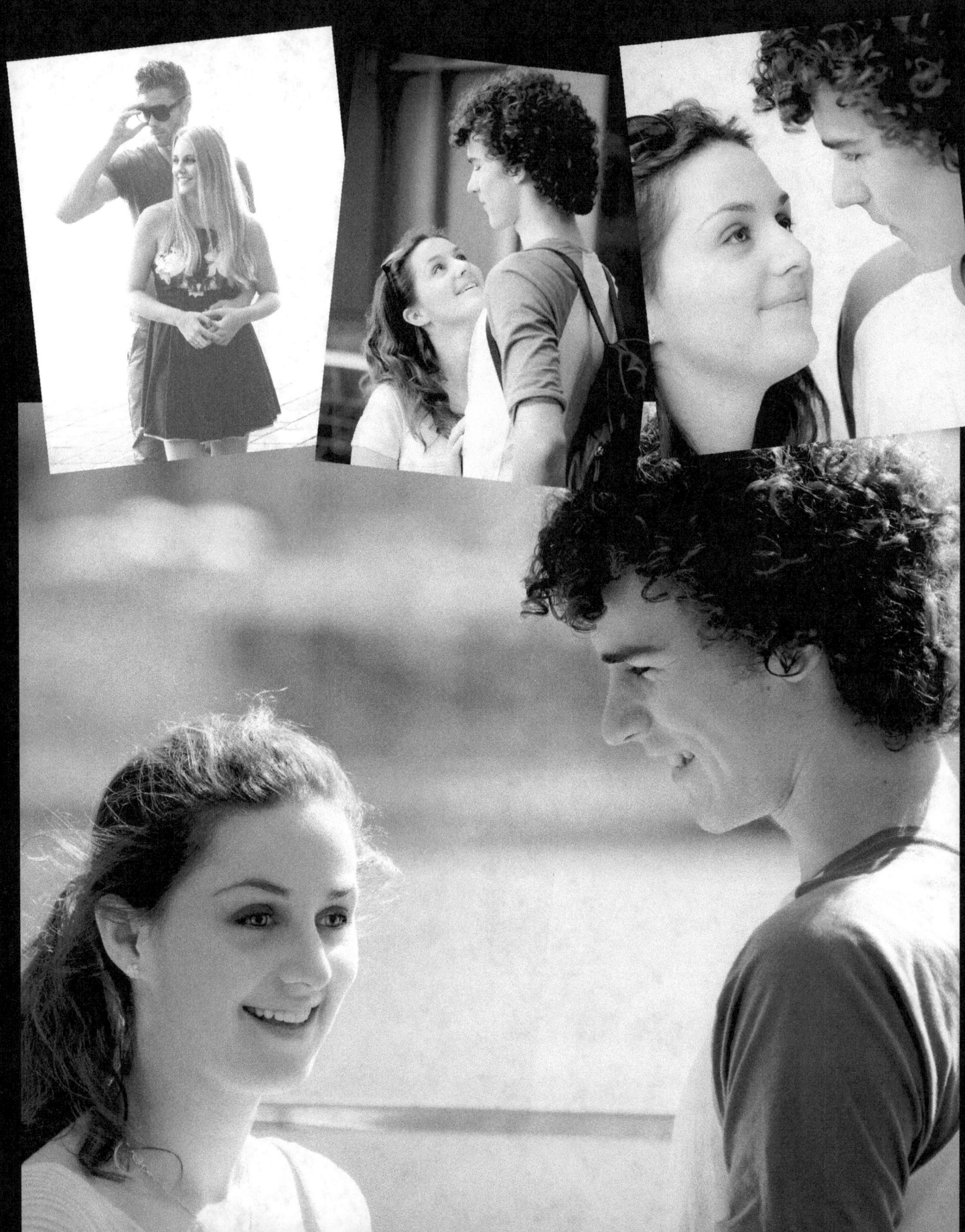

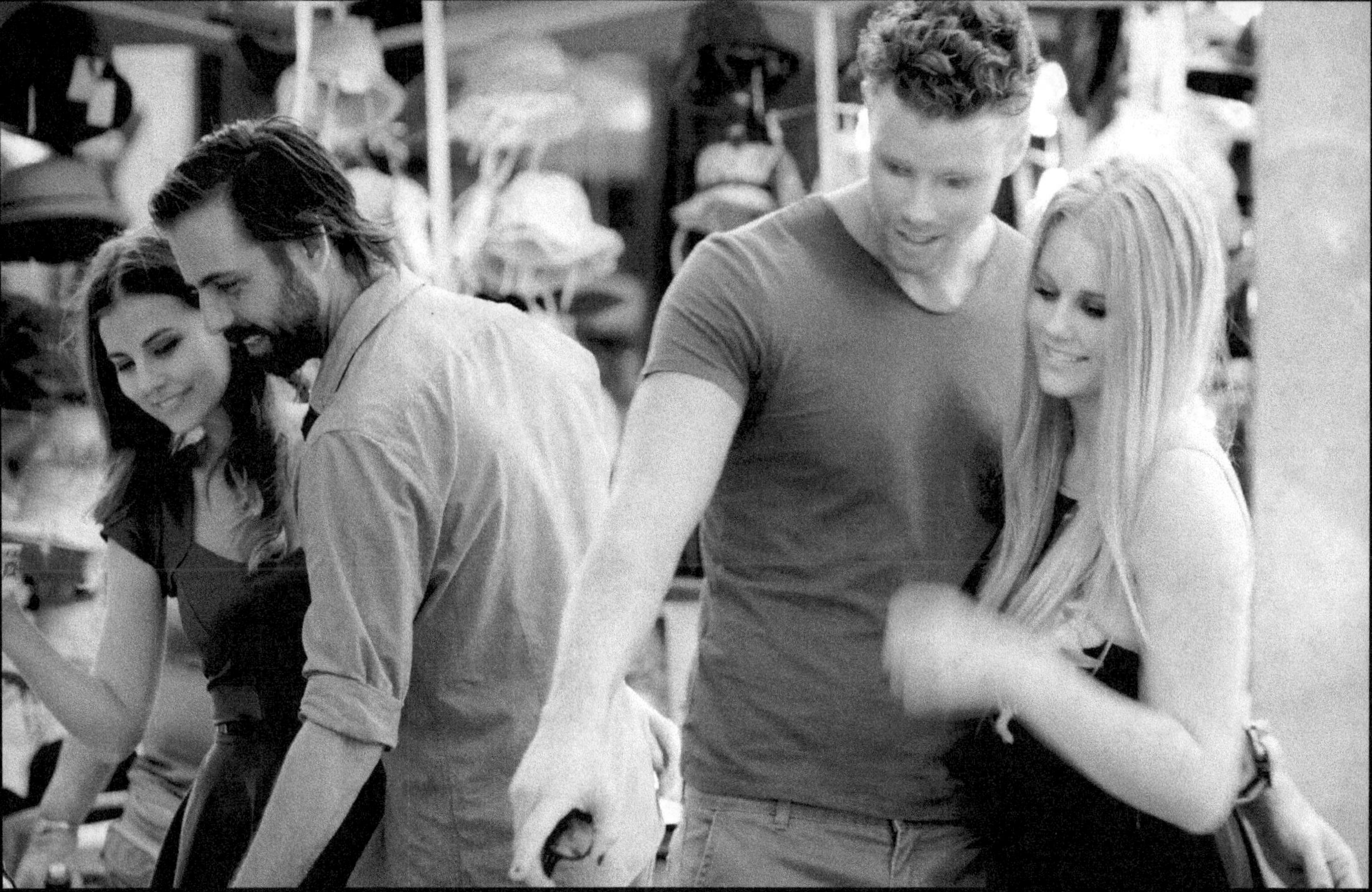

page 21

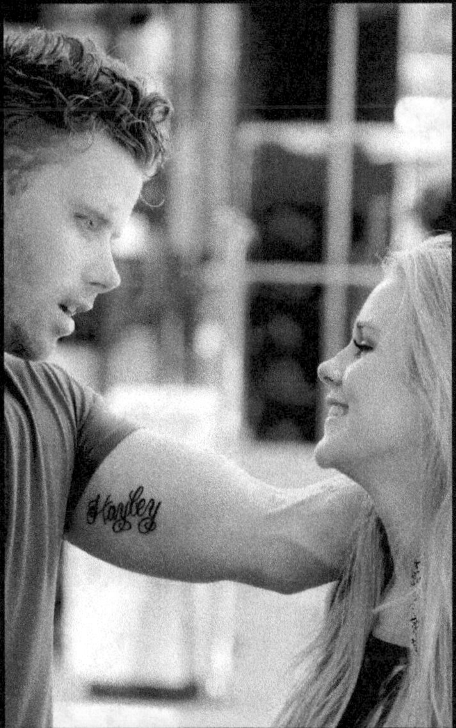

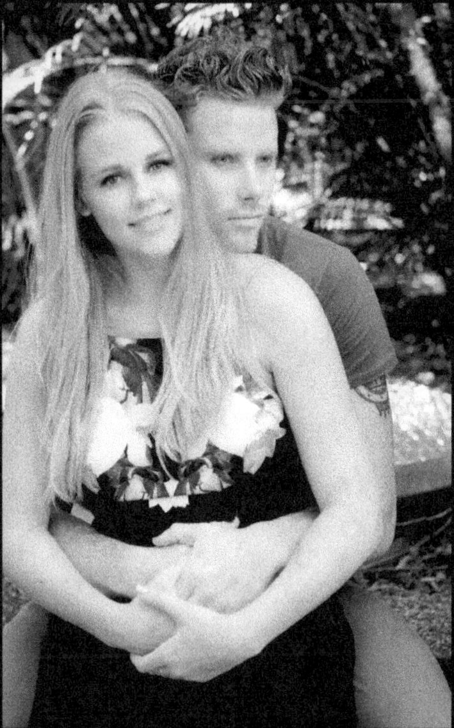

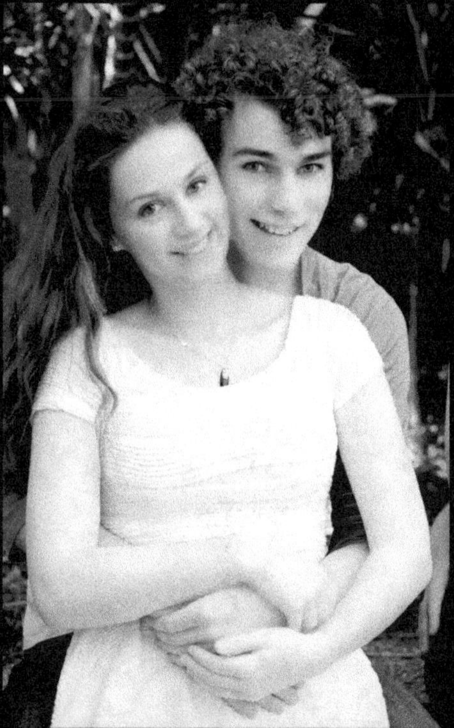

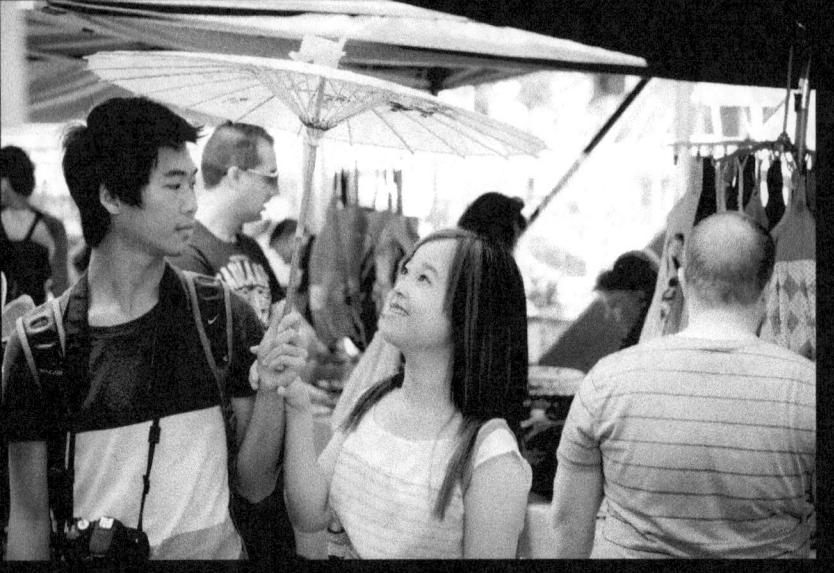

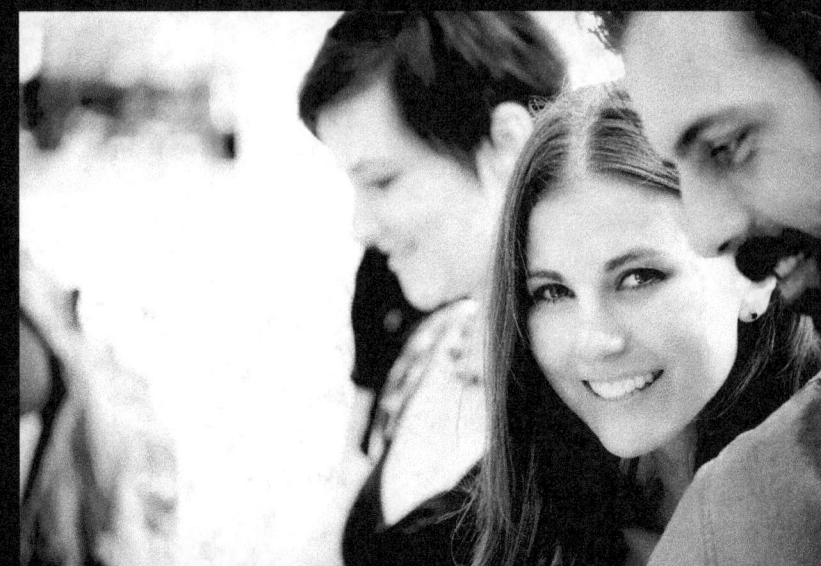

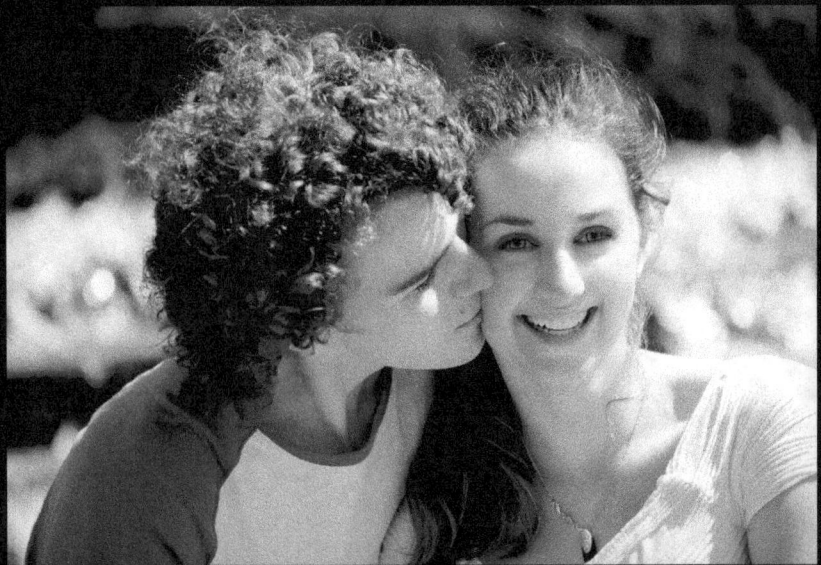

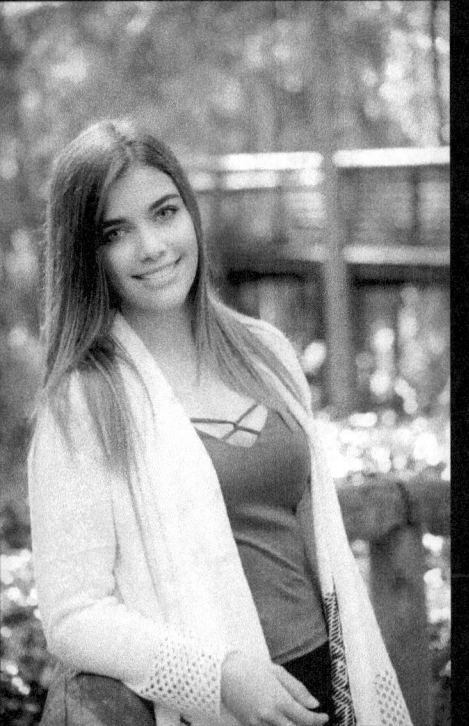
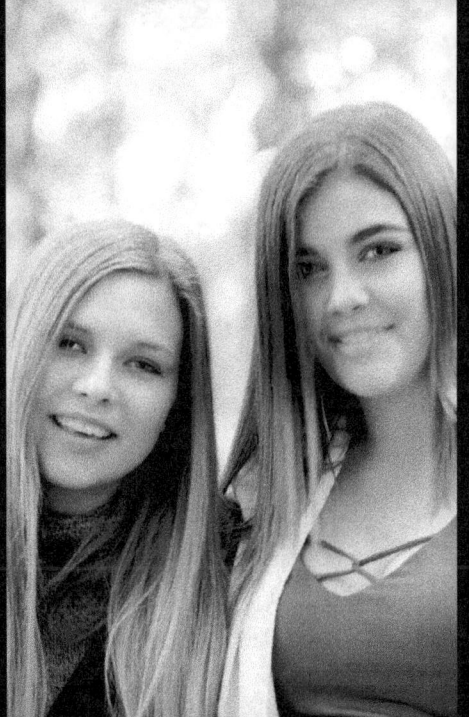
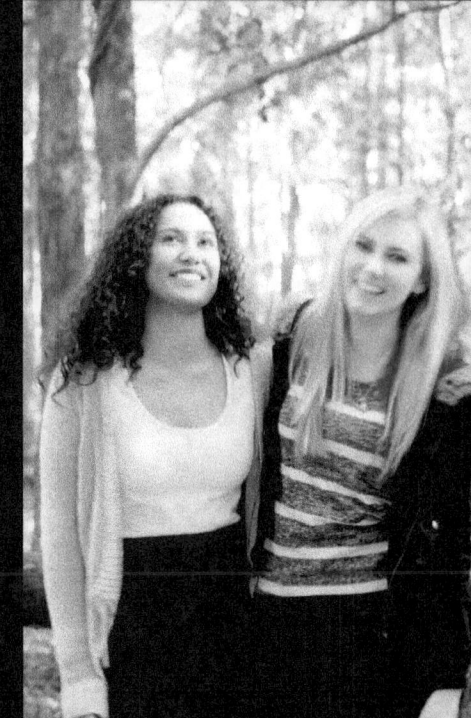

Daisy Hill

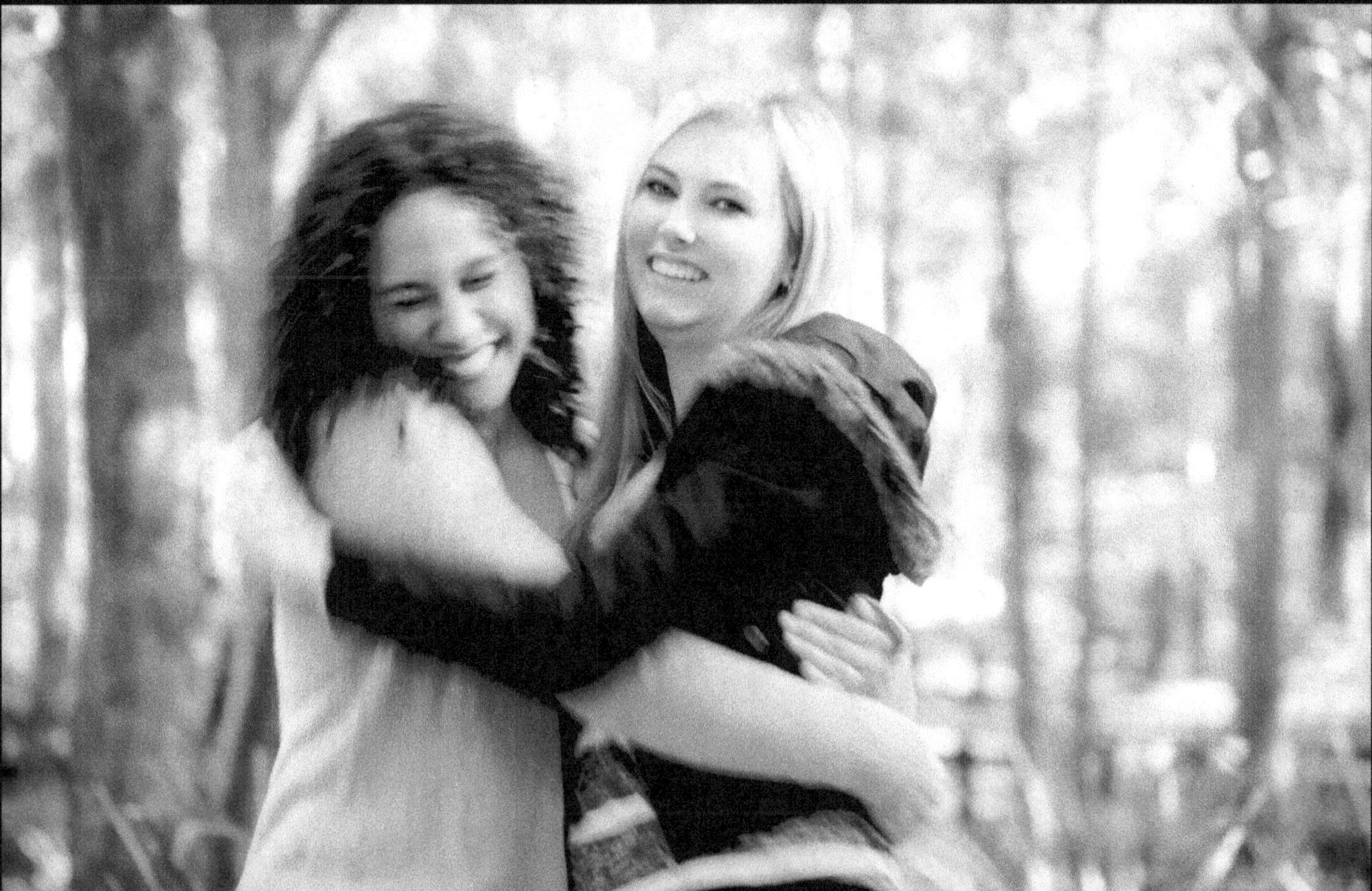

page 23

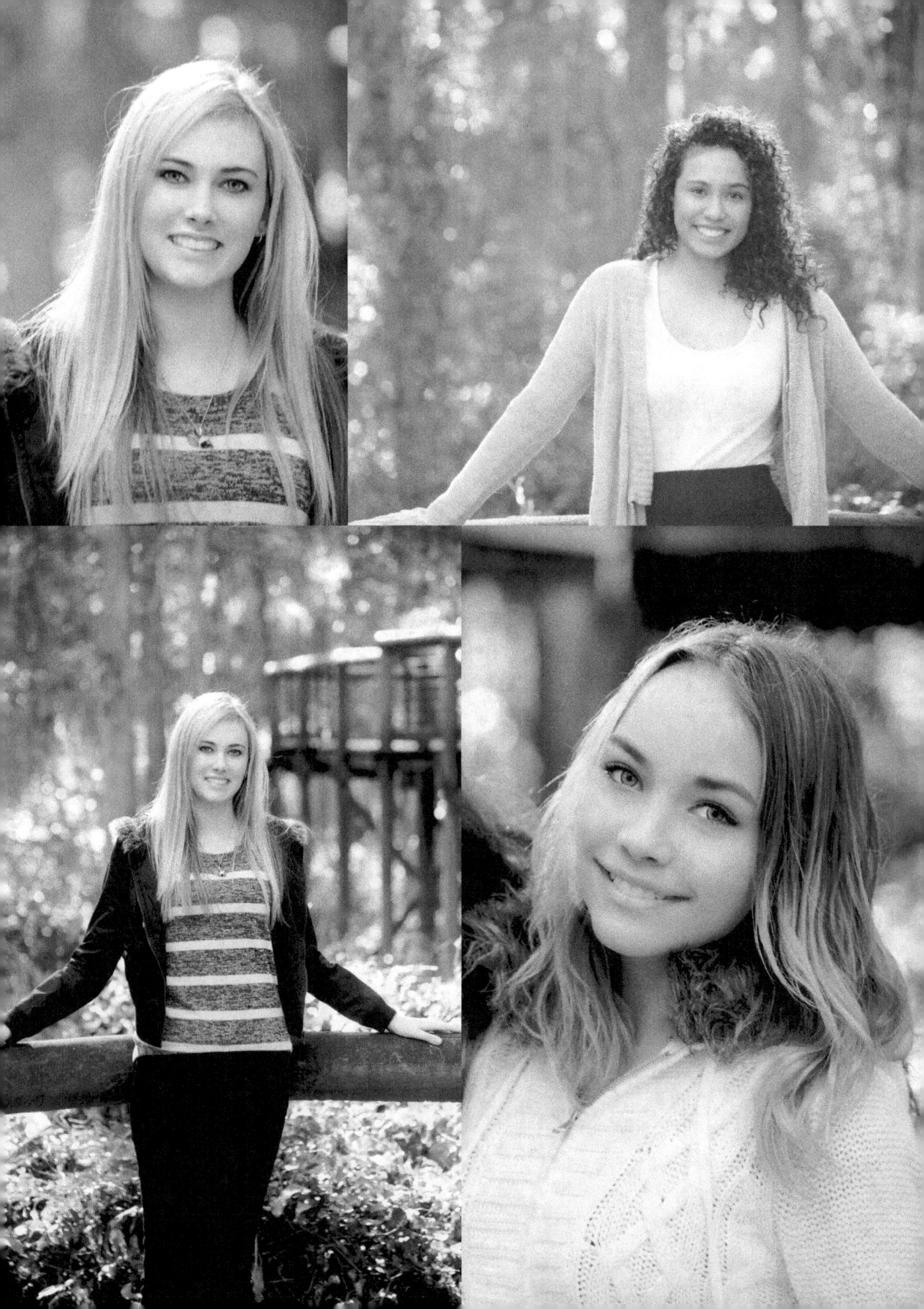

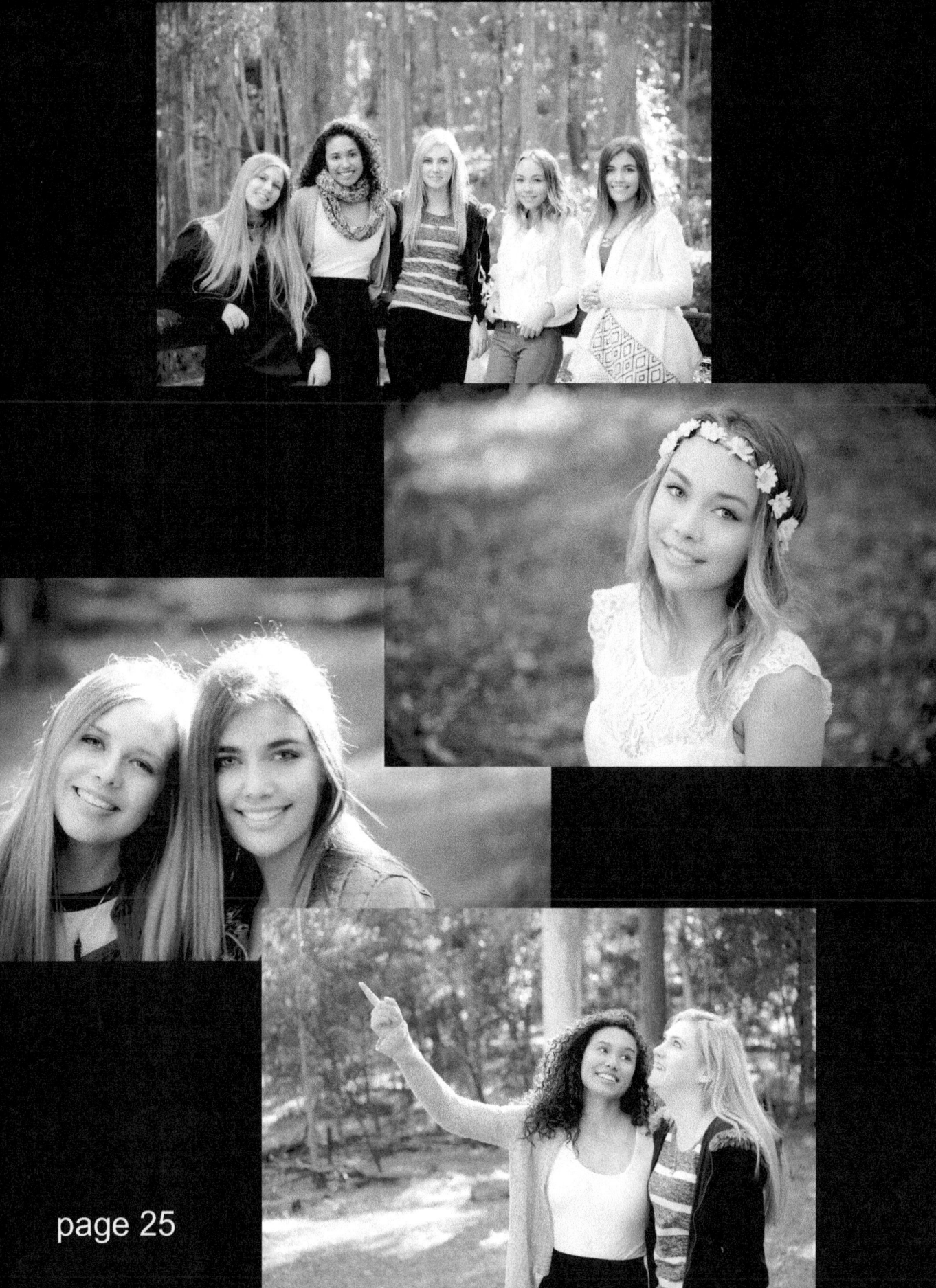

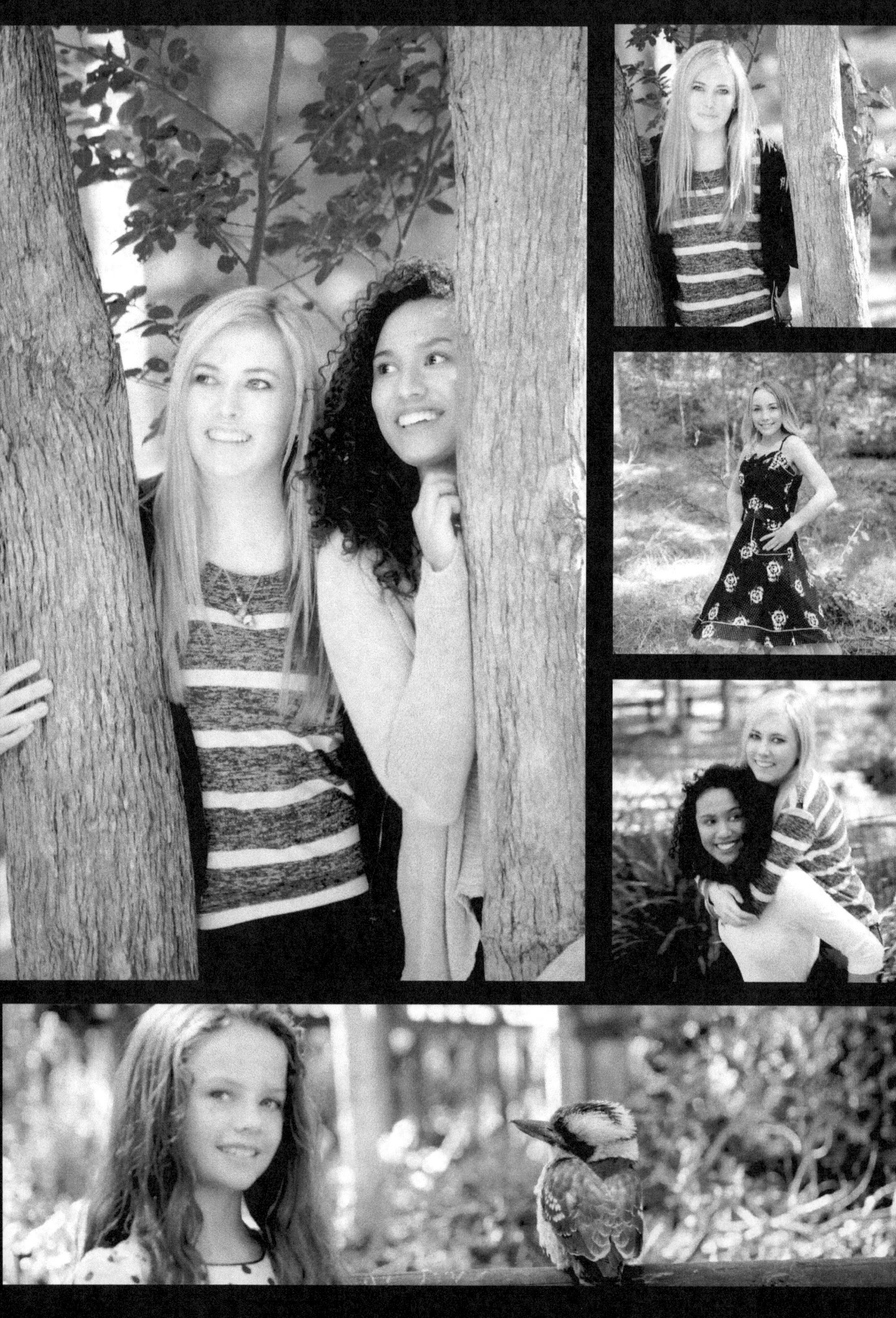

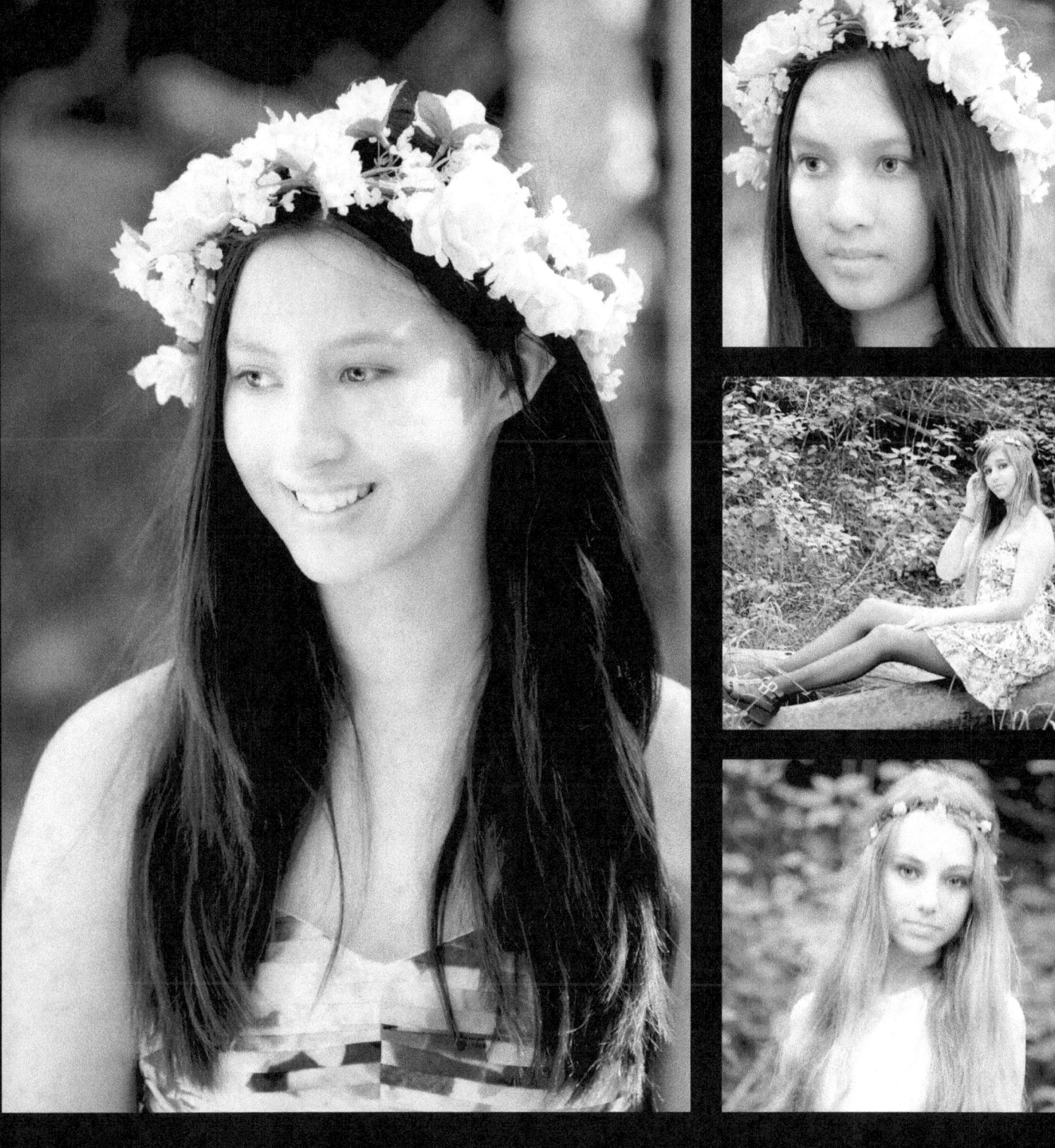

"Fairies in the Forest" shoot at
Brisbane Forest Park.

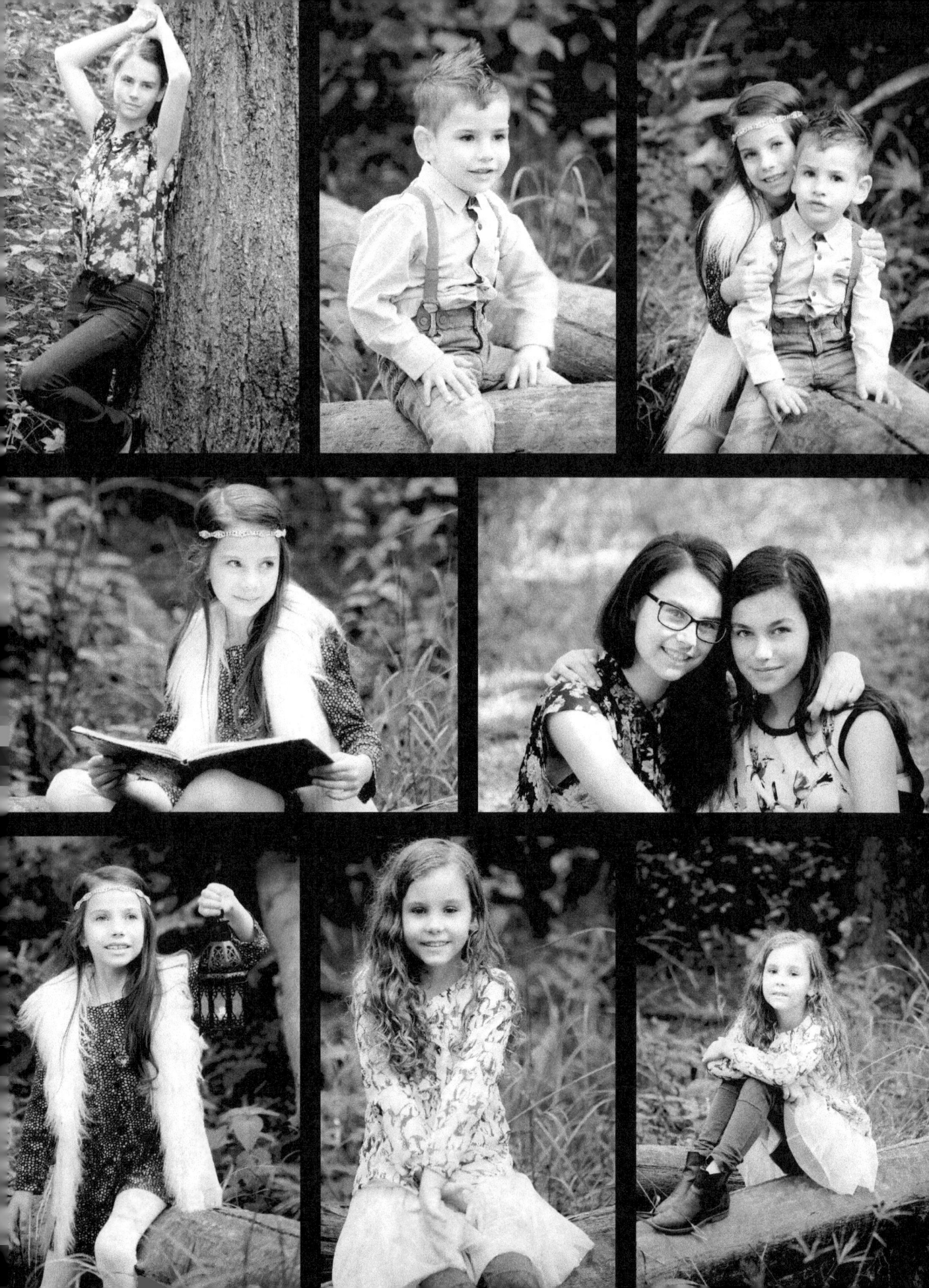

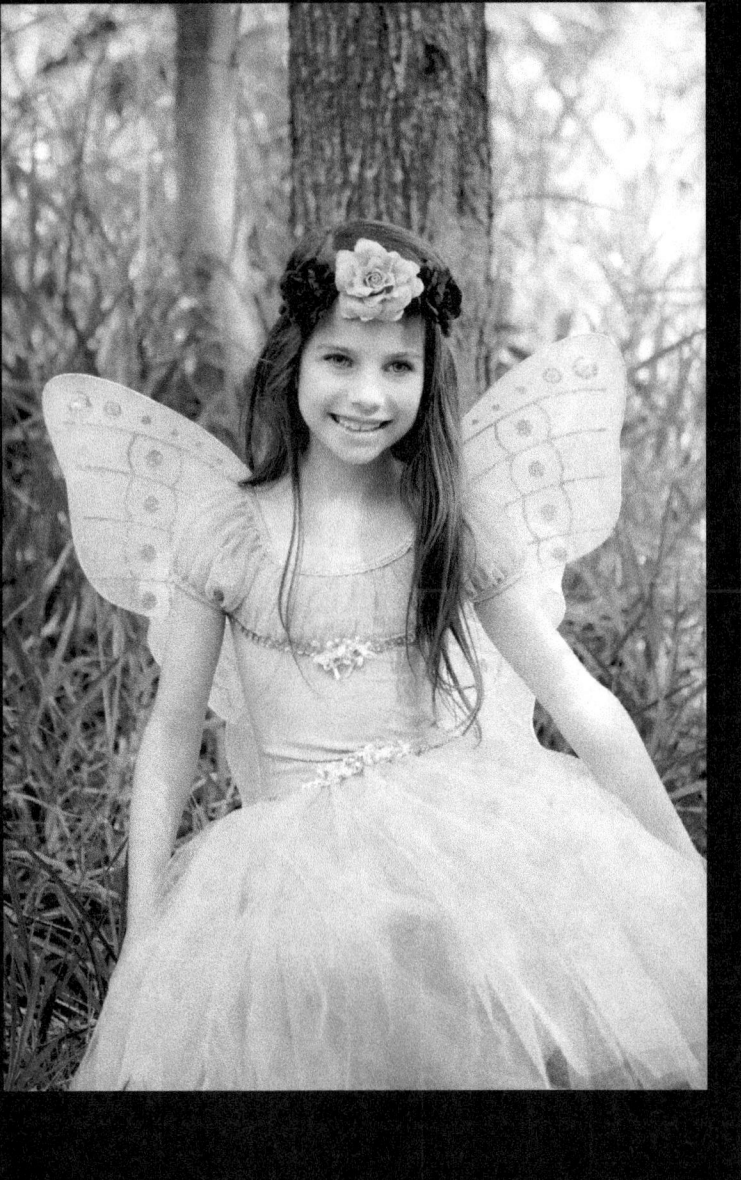

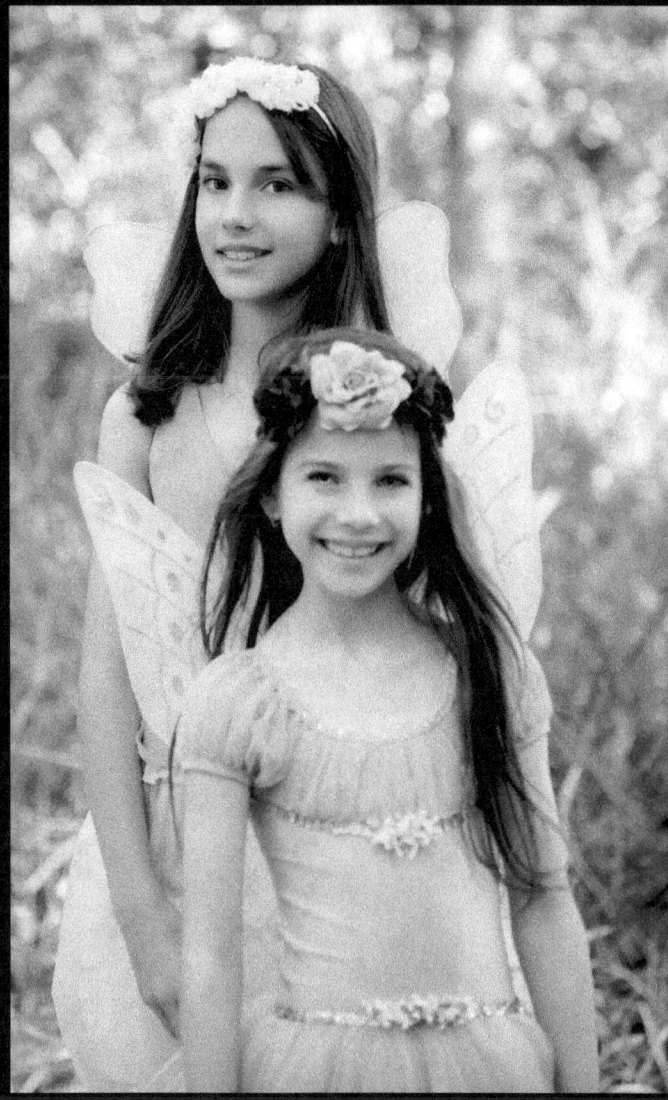

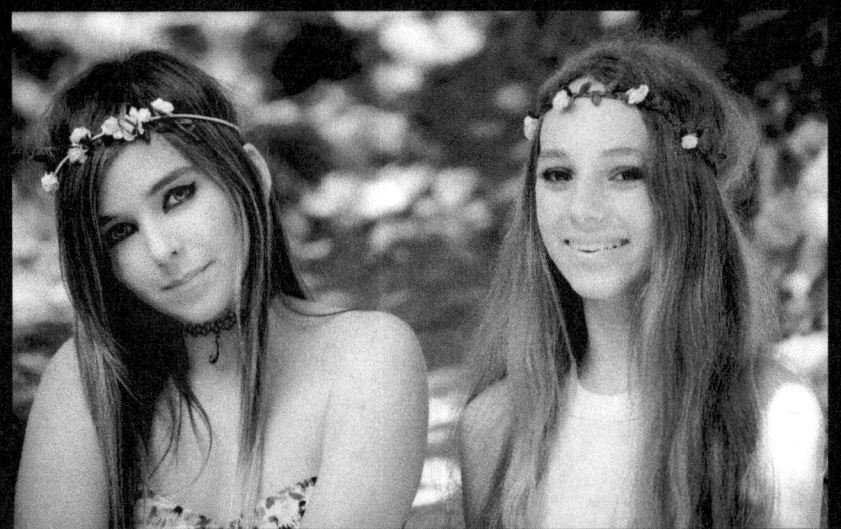

page 29

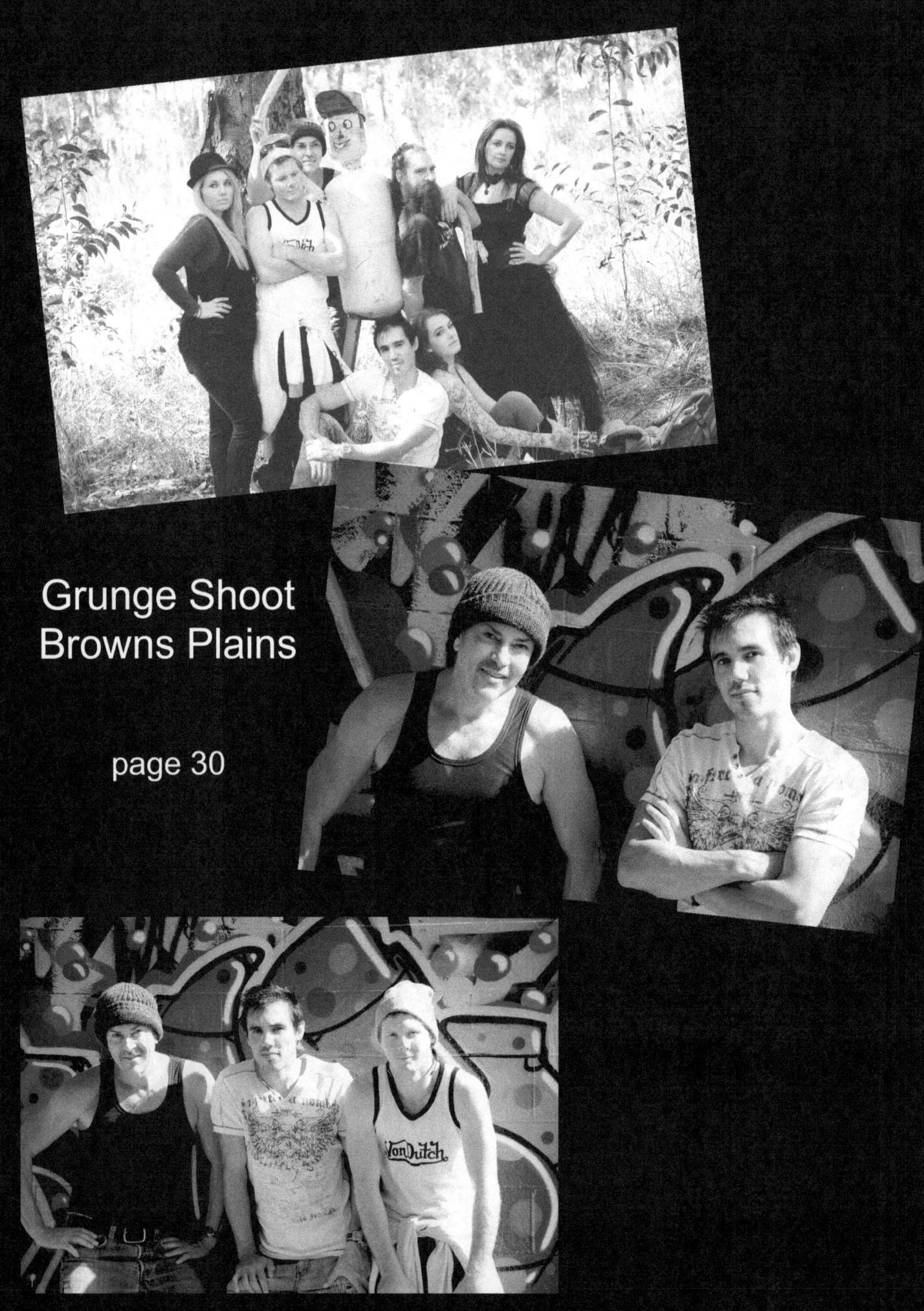

Grunge Shoot
Browns Plains

page 30

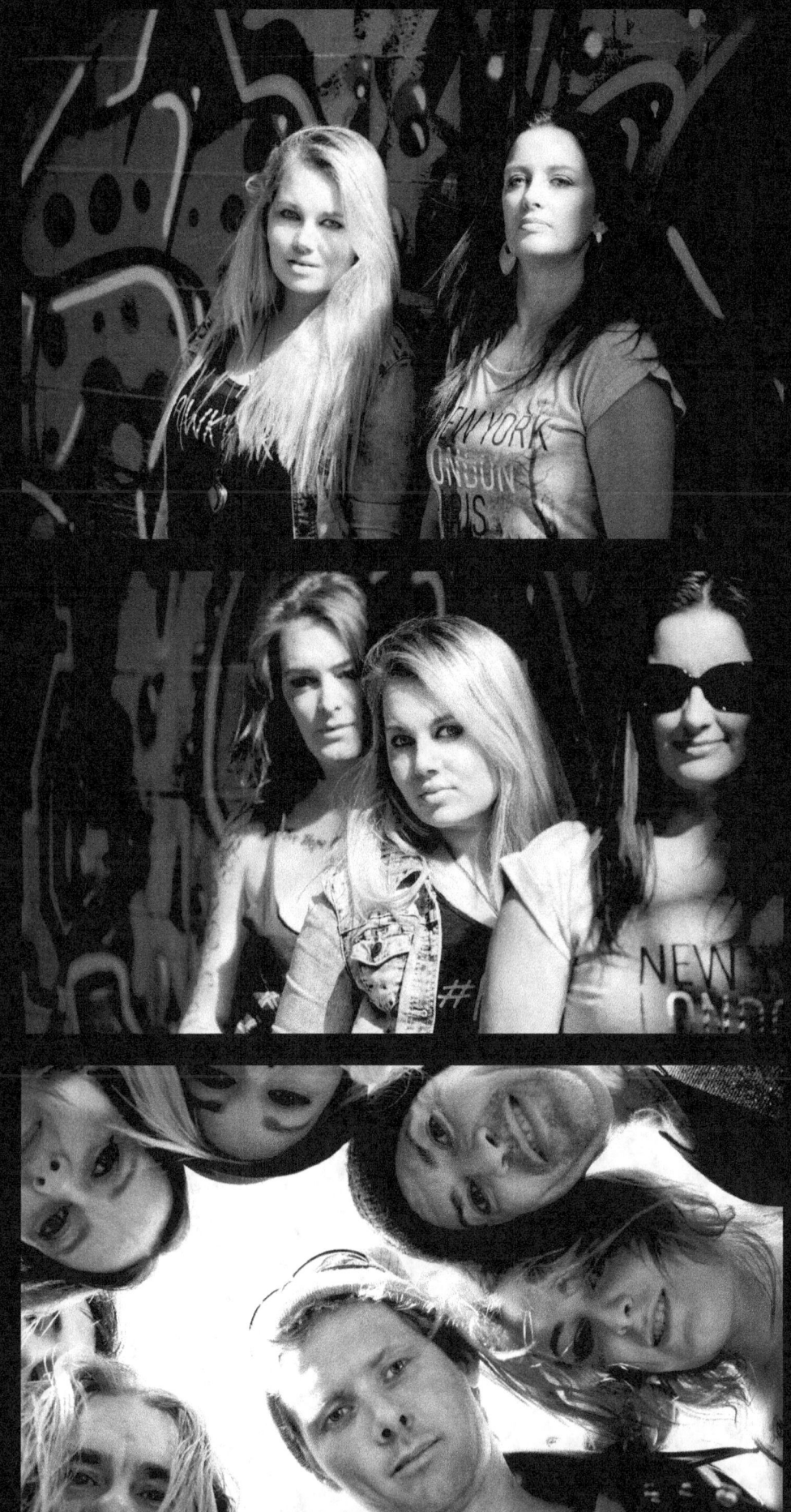

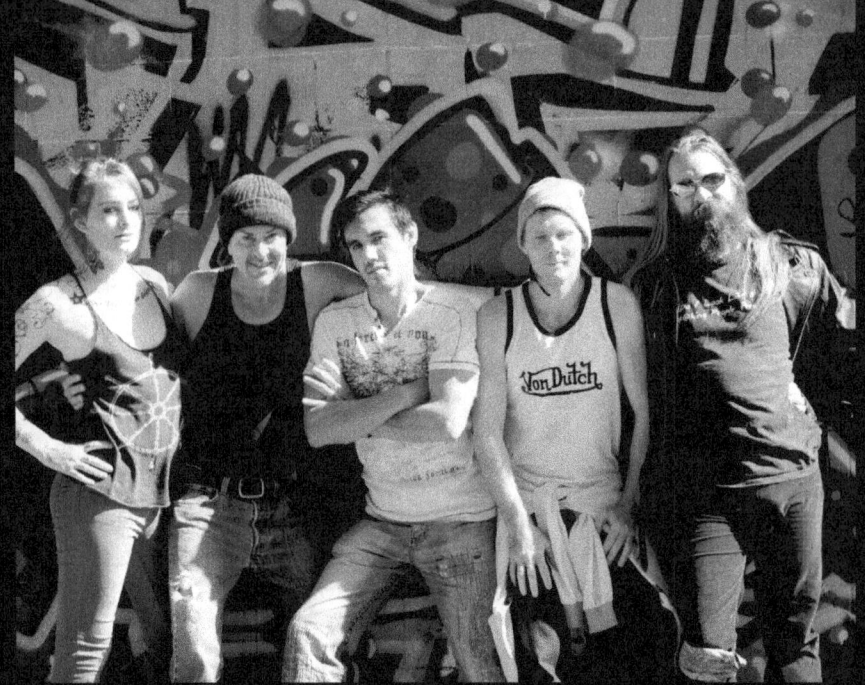

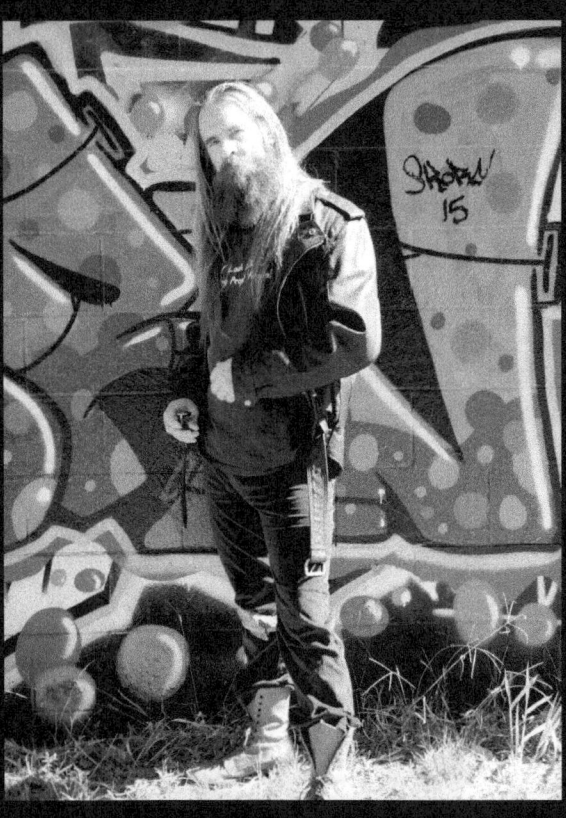

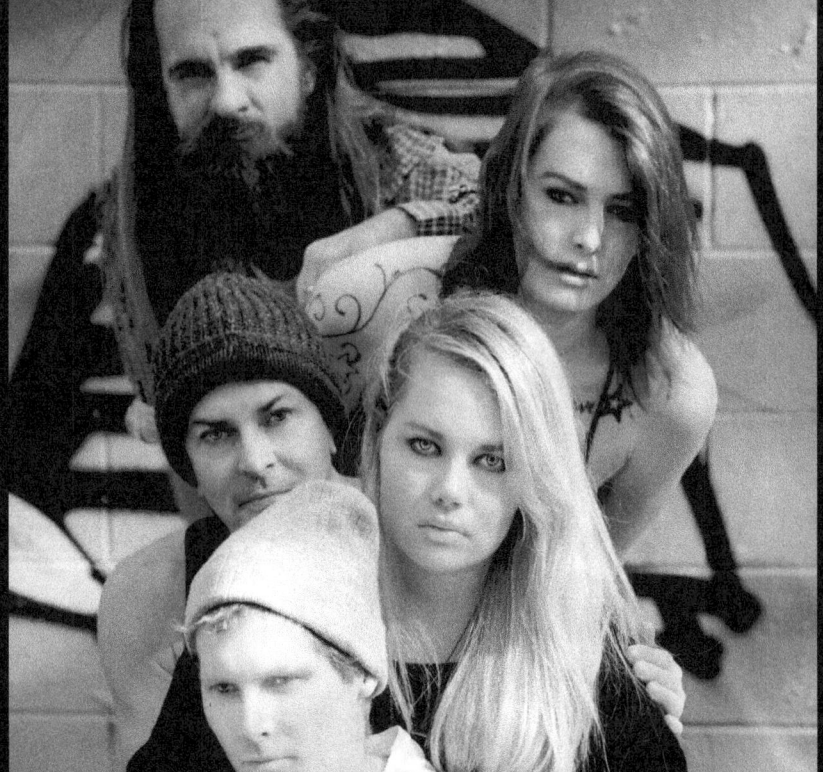

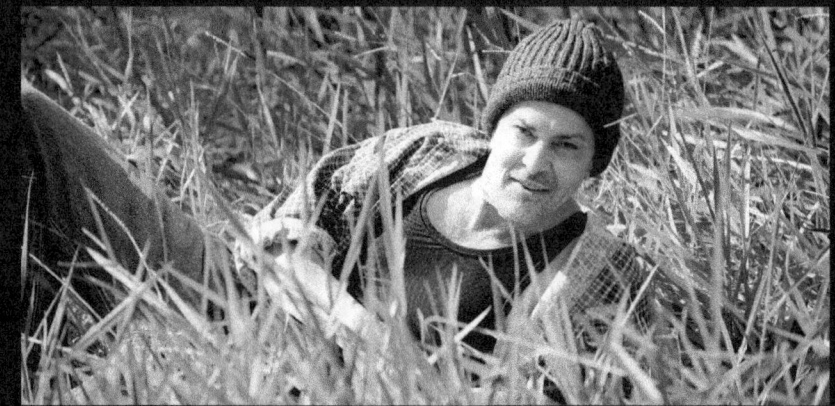

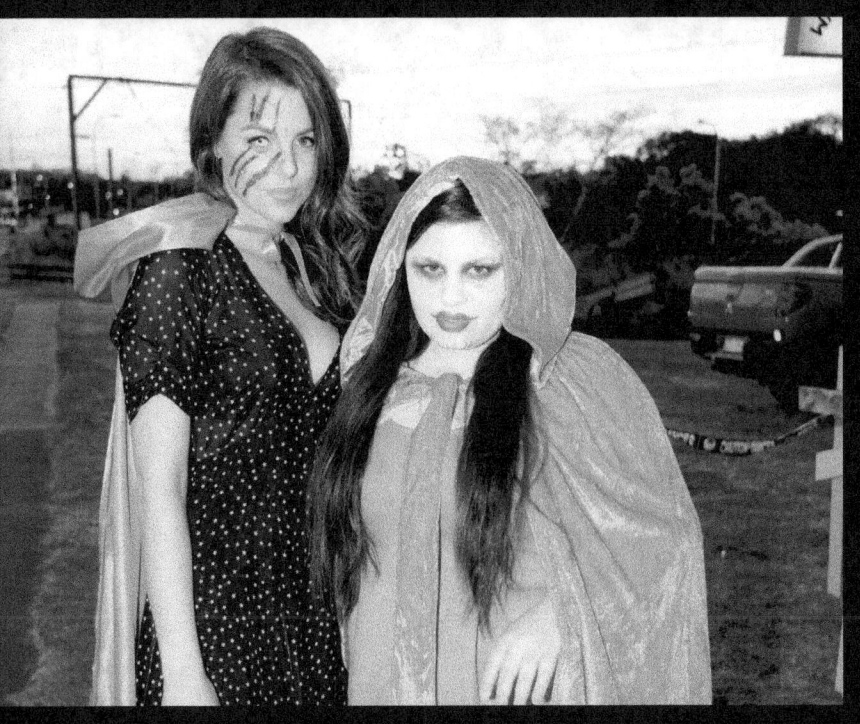

Halloween
Shoot

page 33

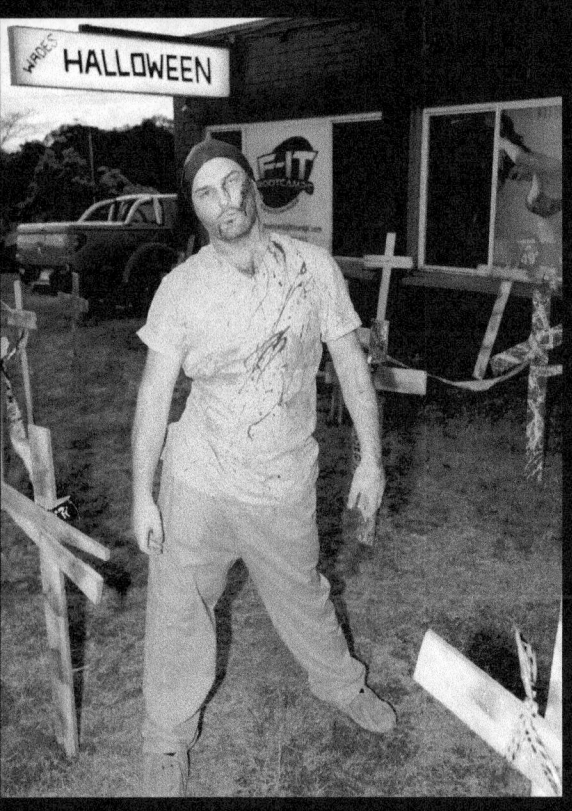

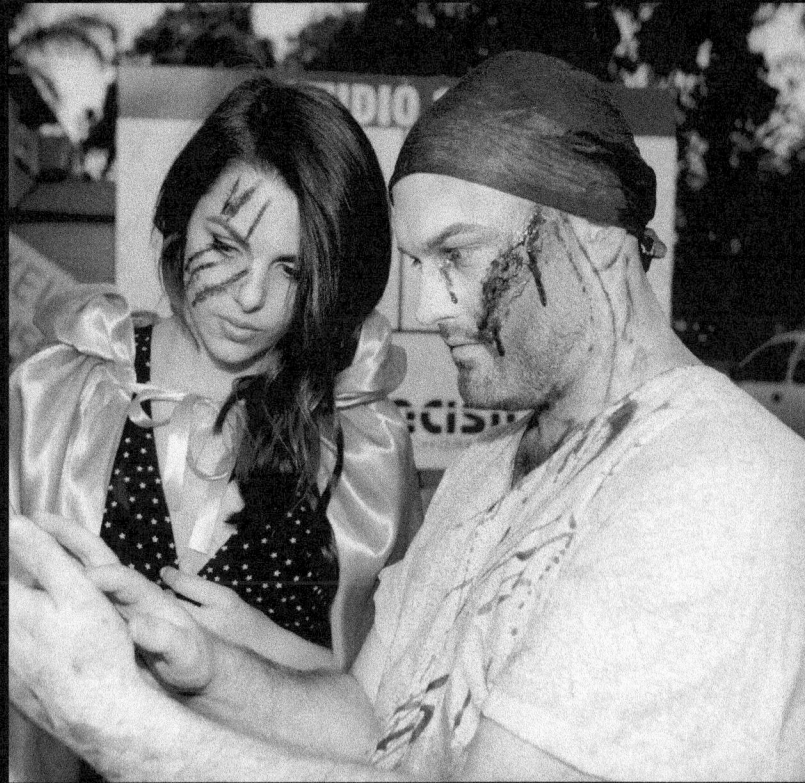

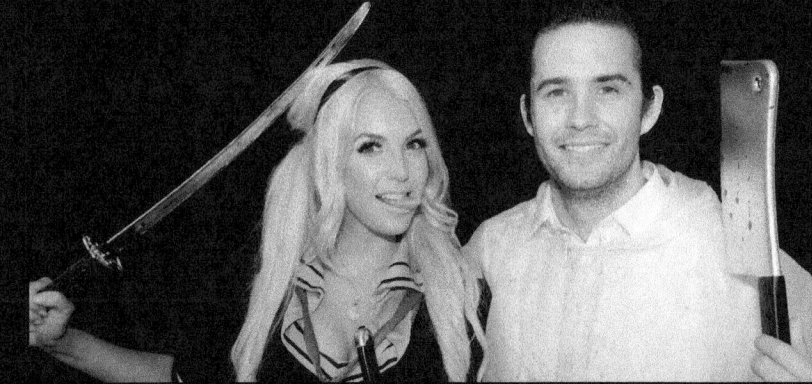

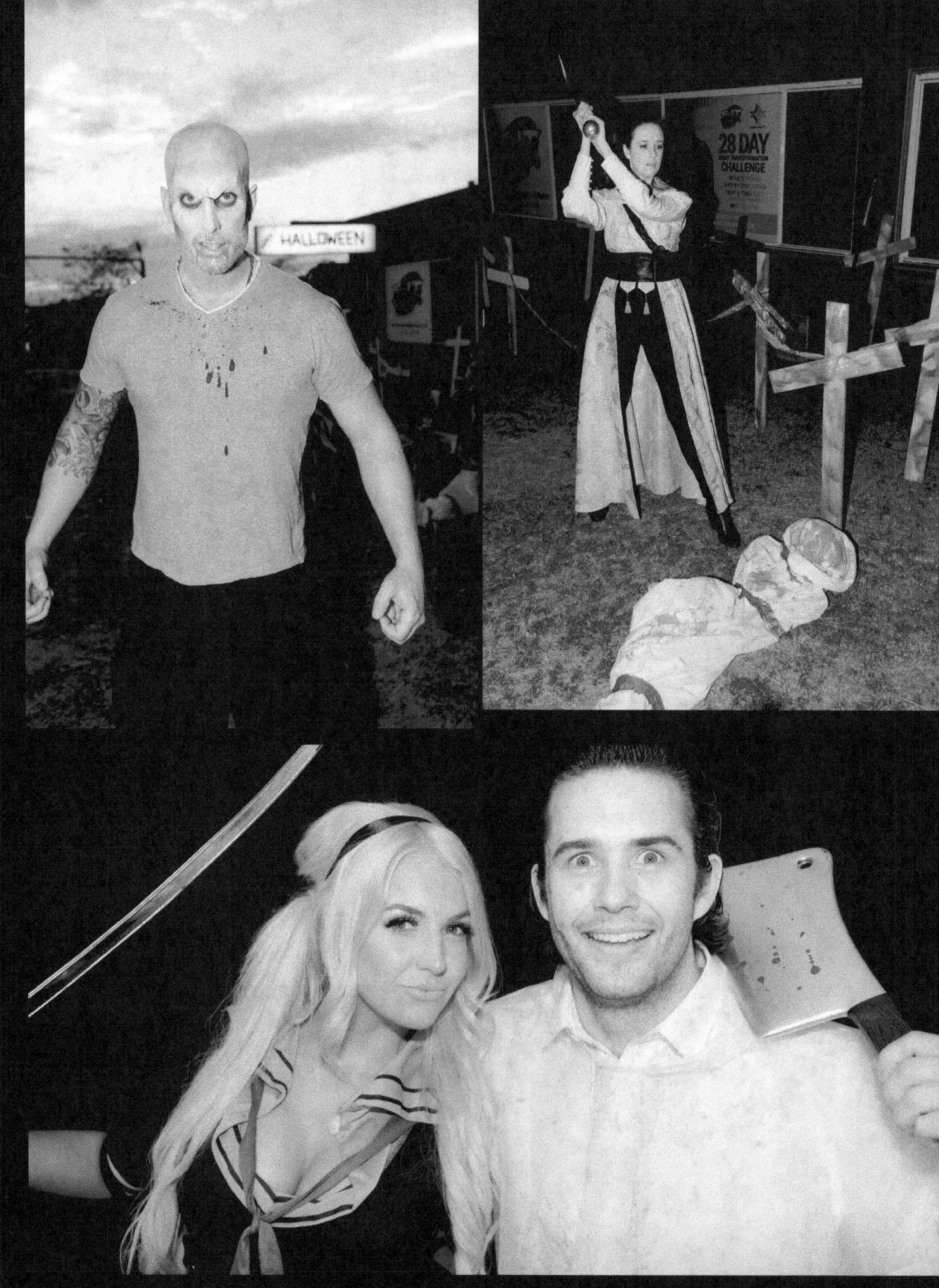

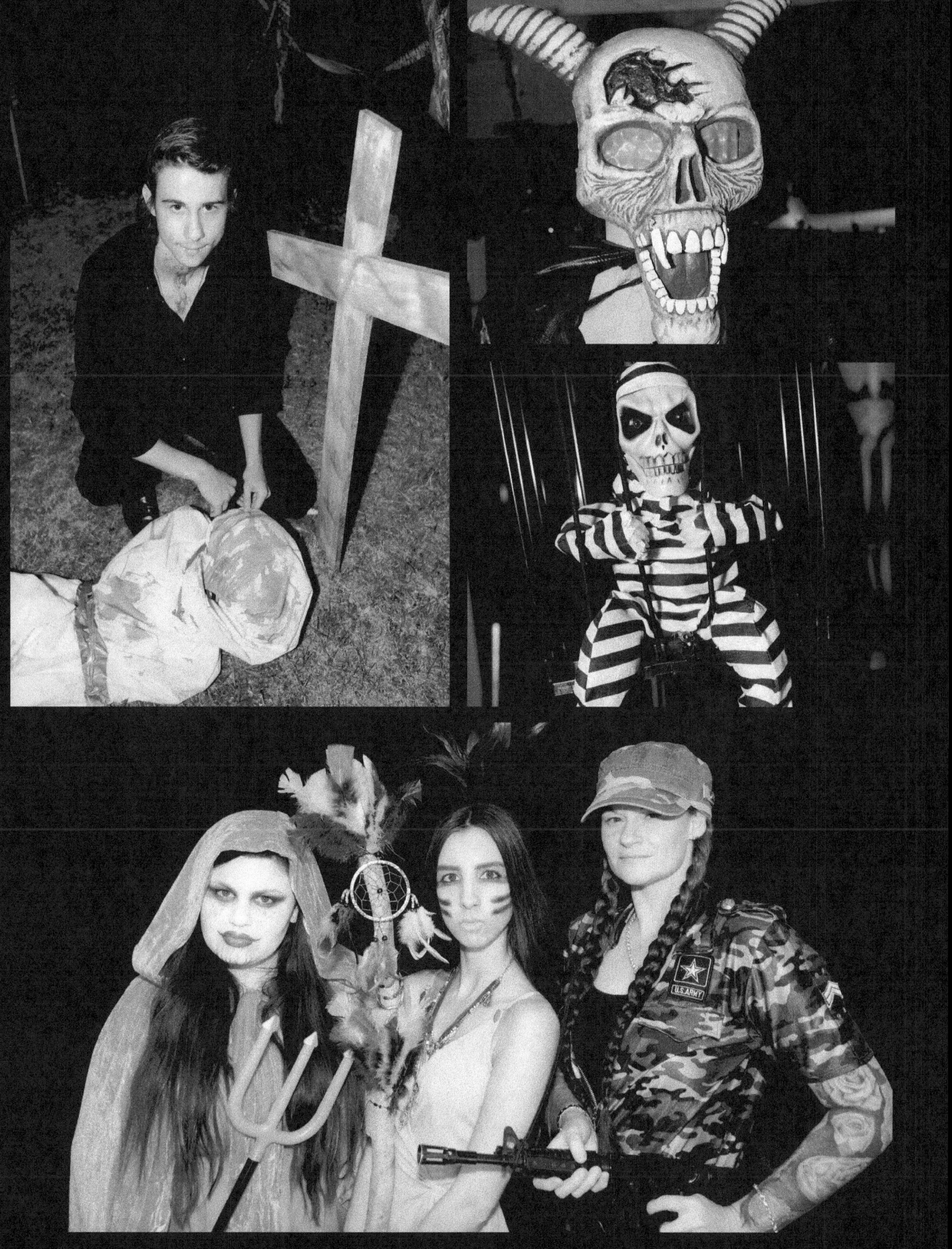

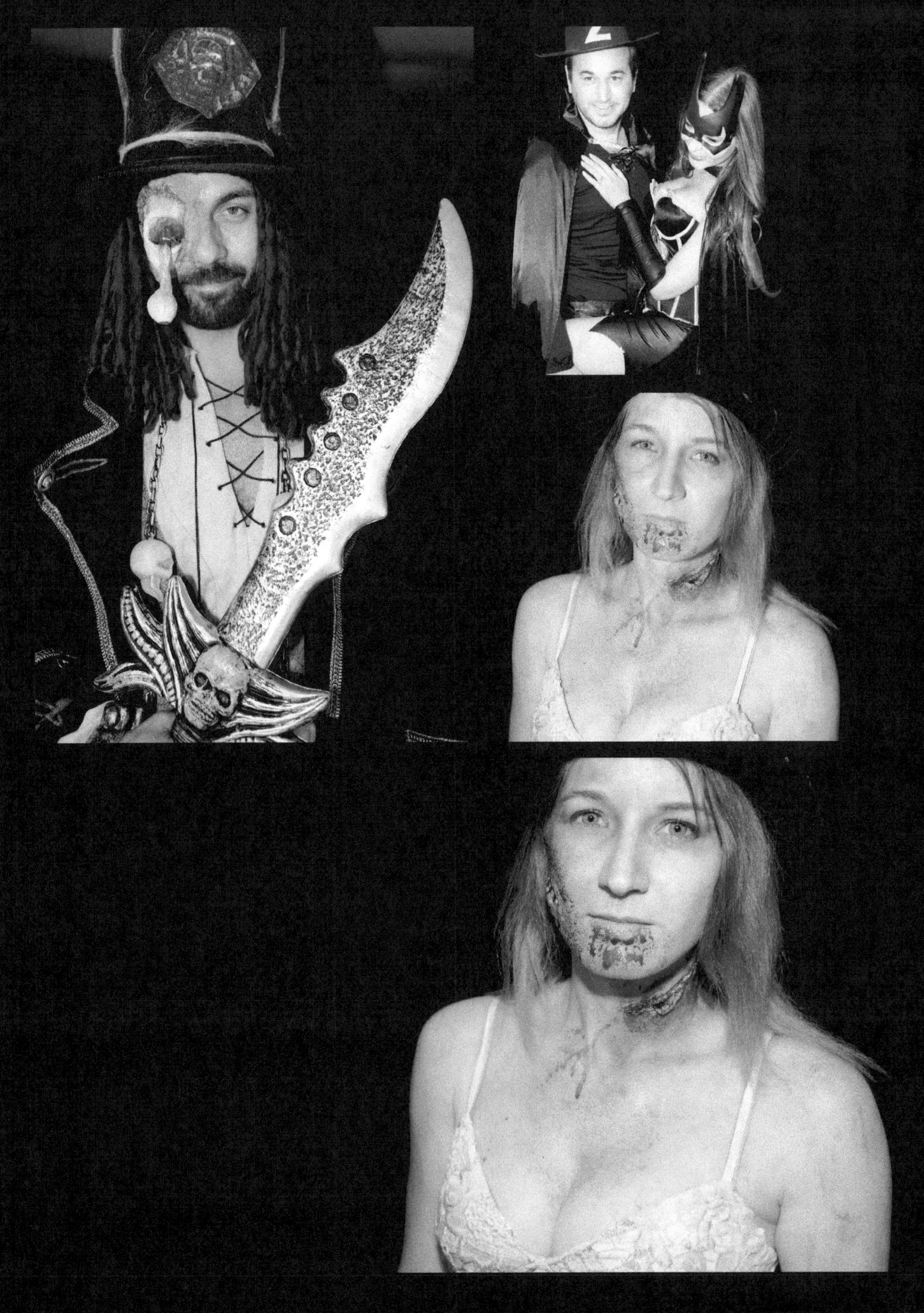

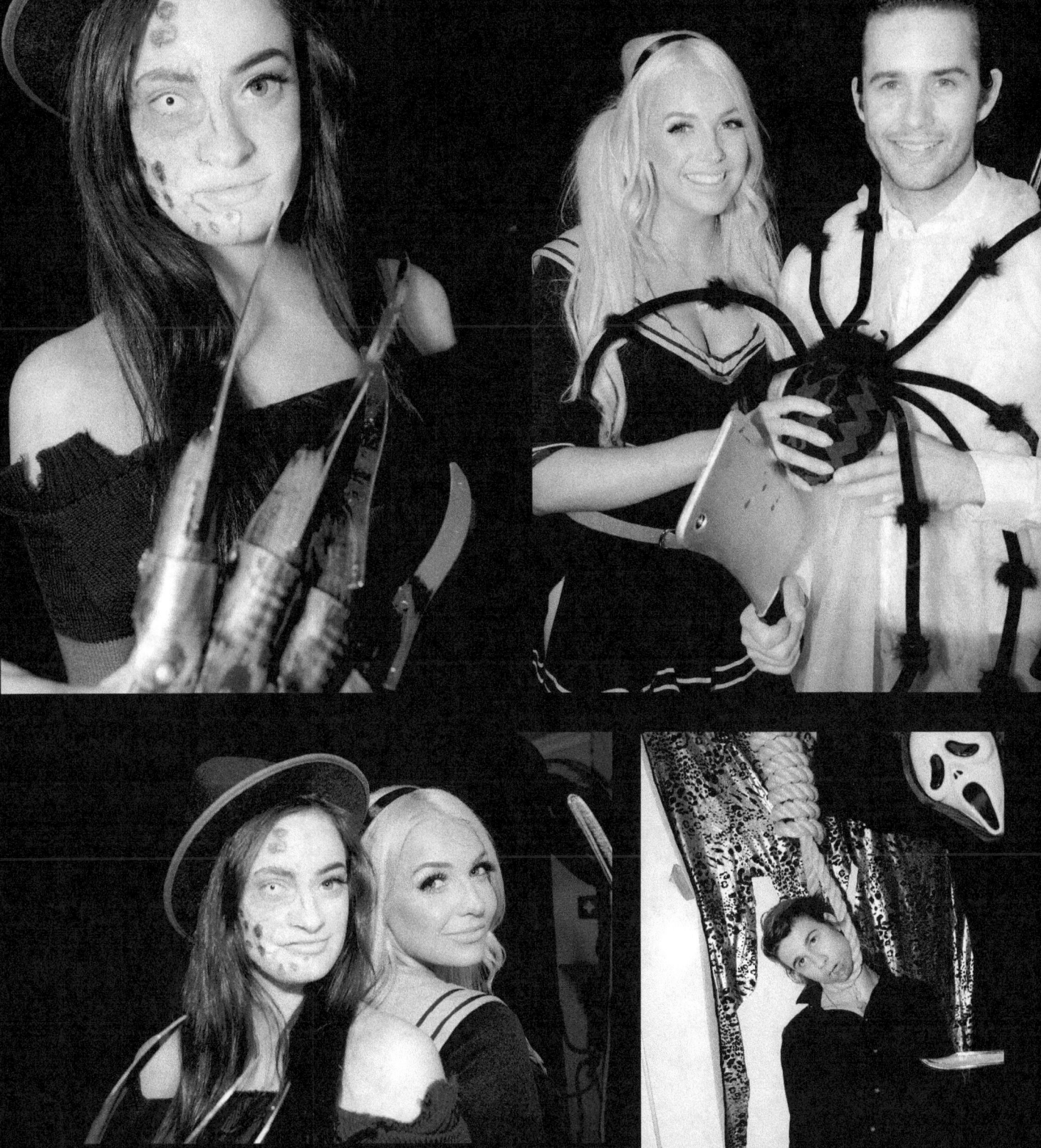

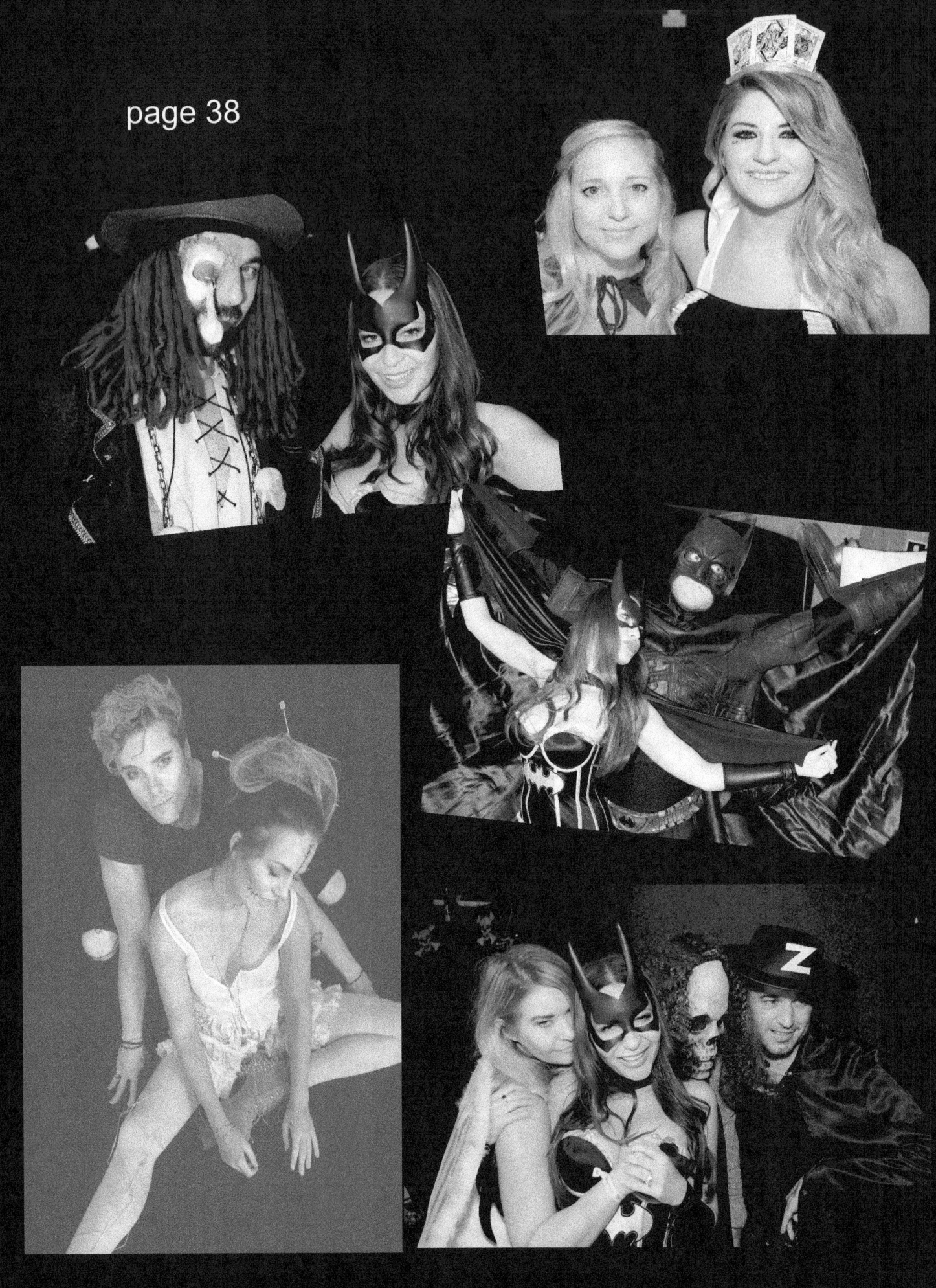

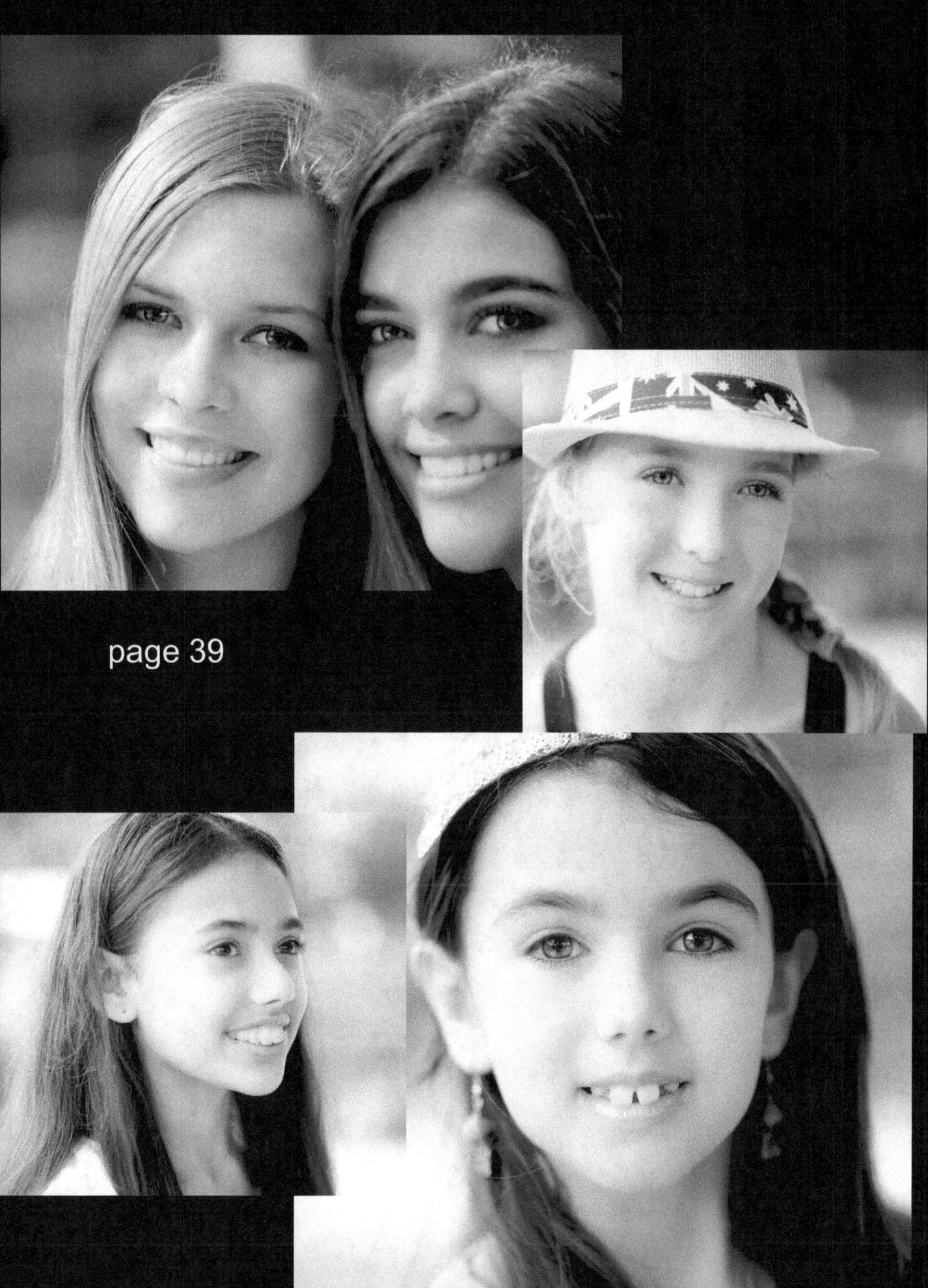

page 39

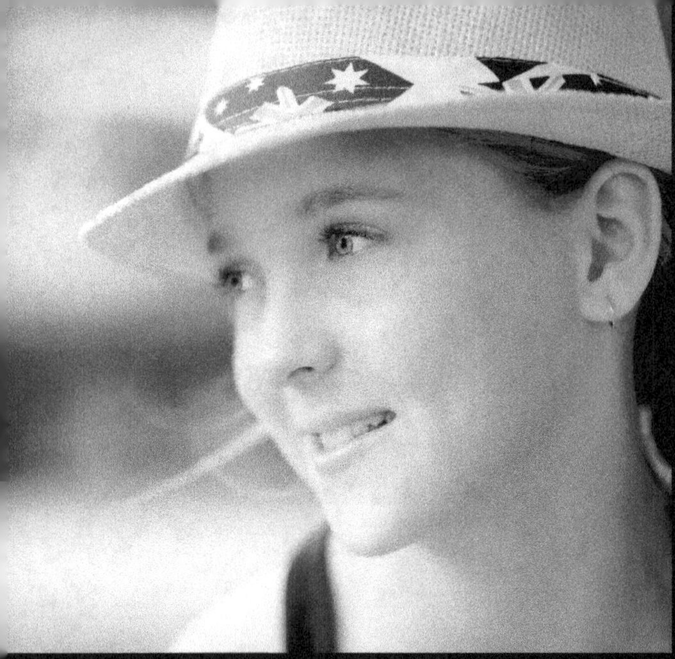

Head Shots

page 40

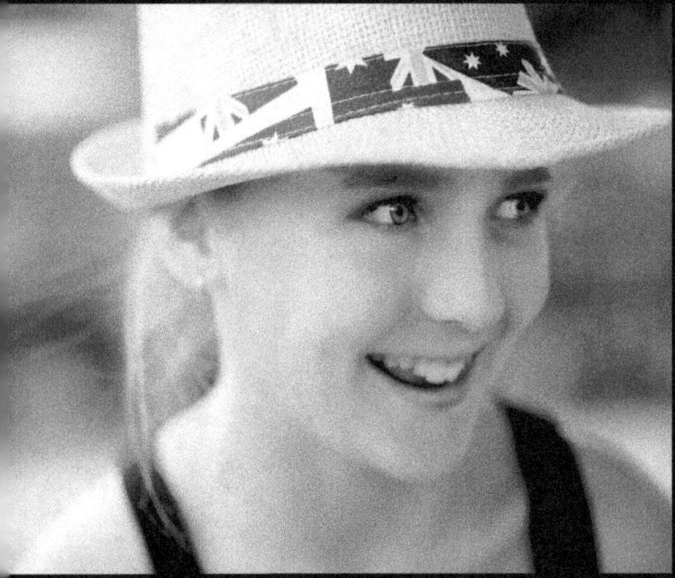

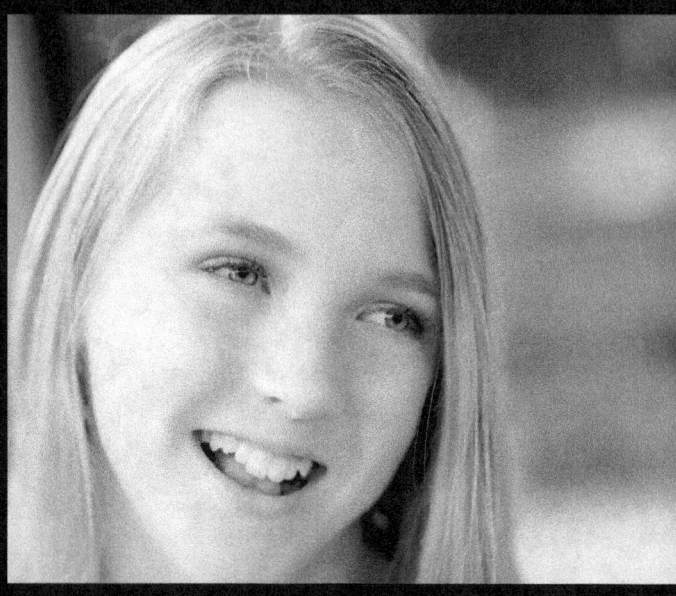
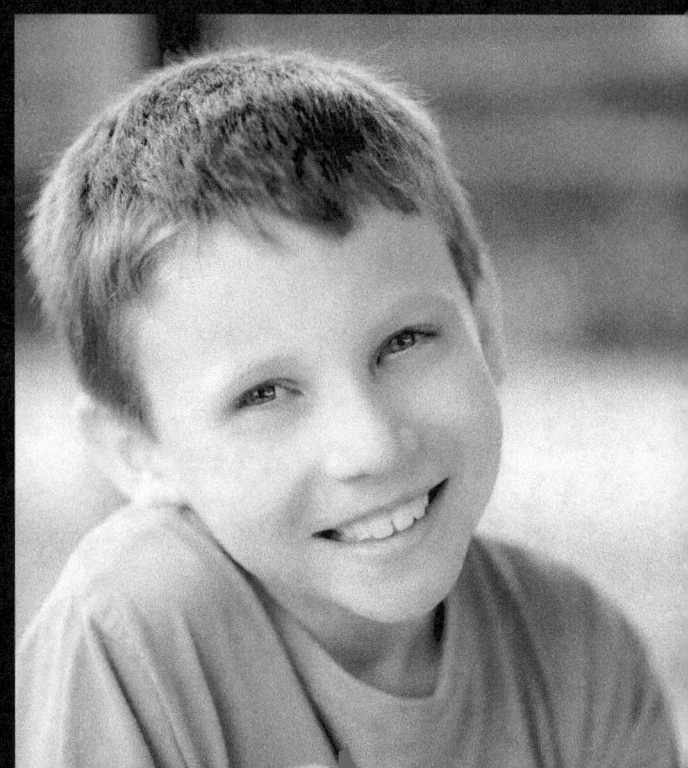

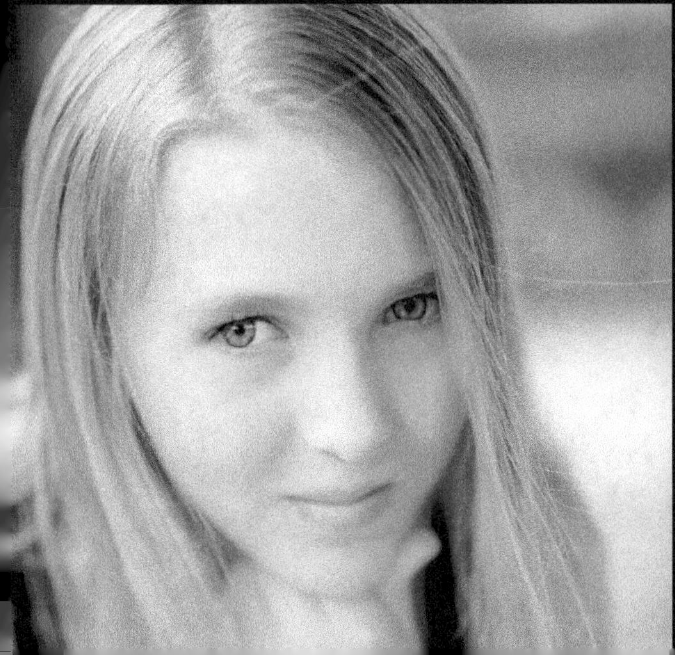

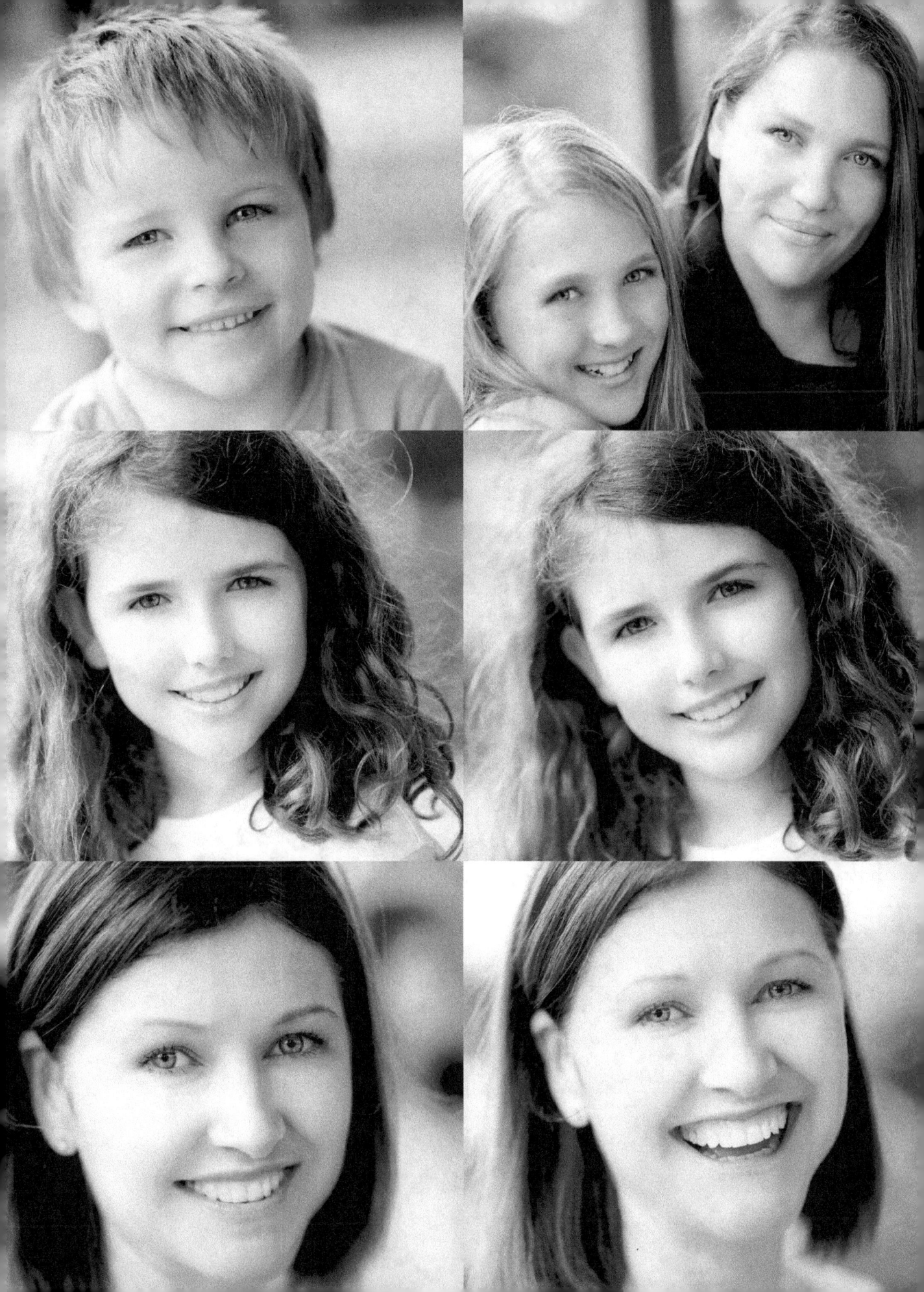

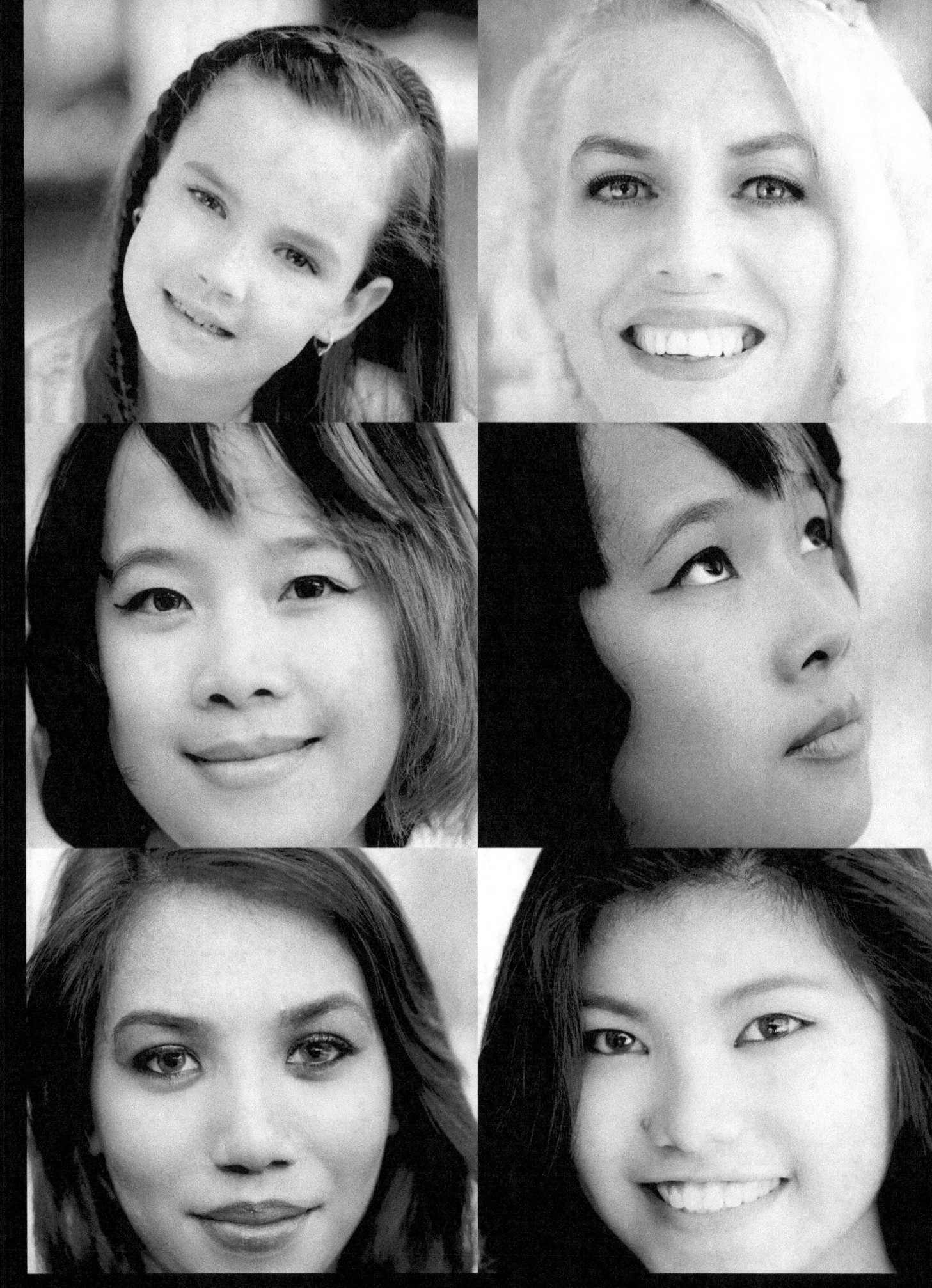

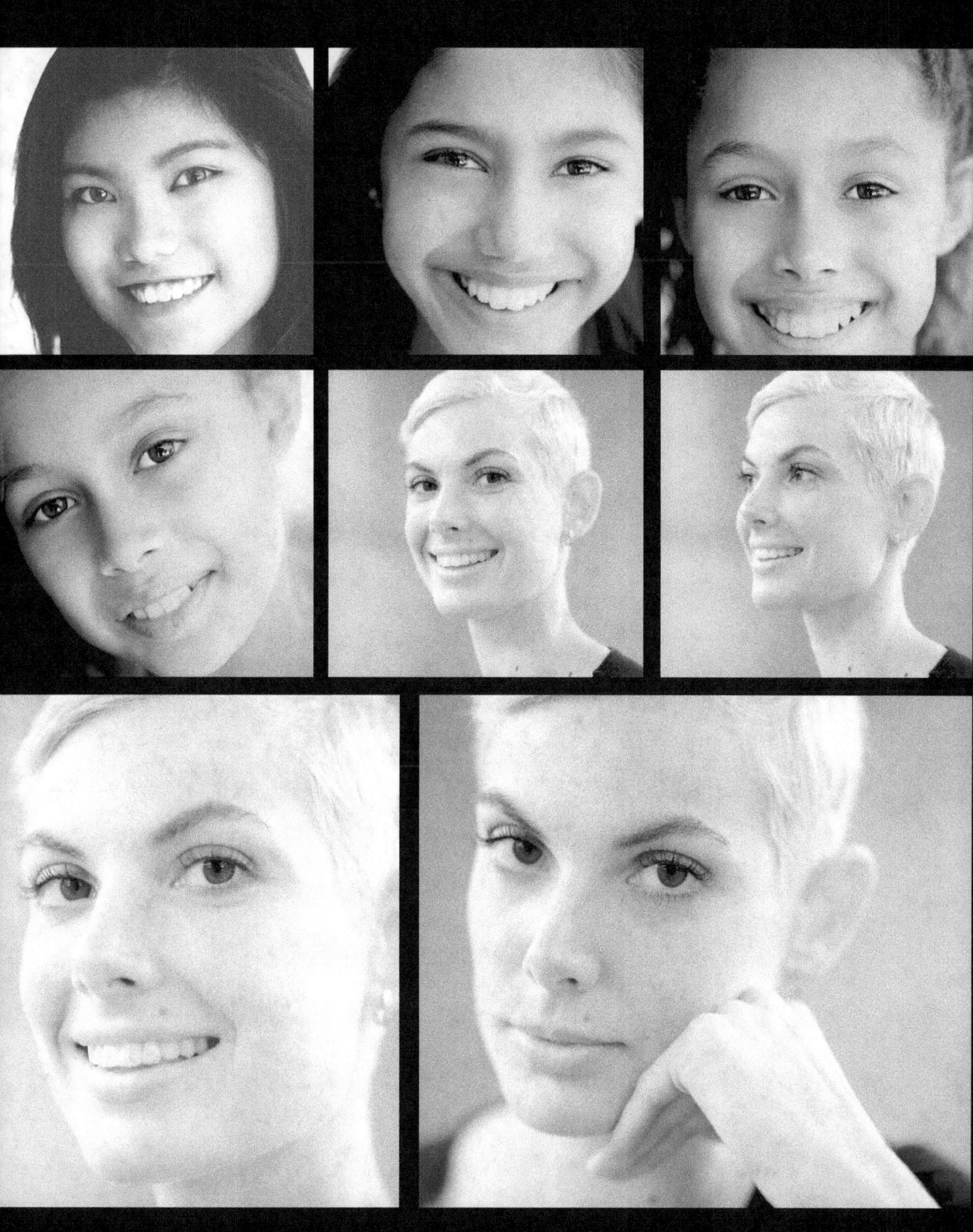

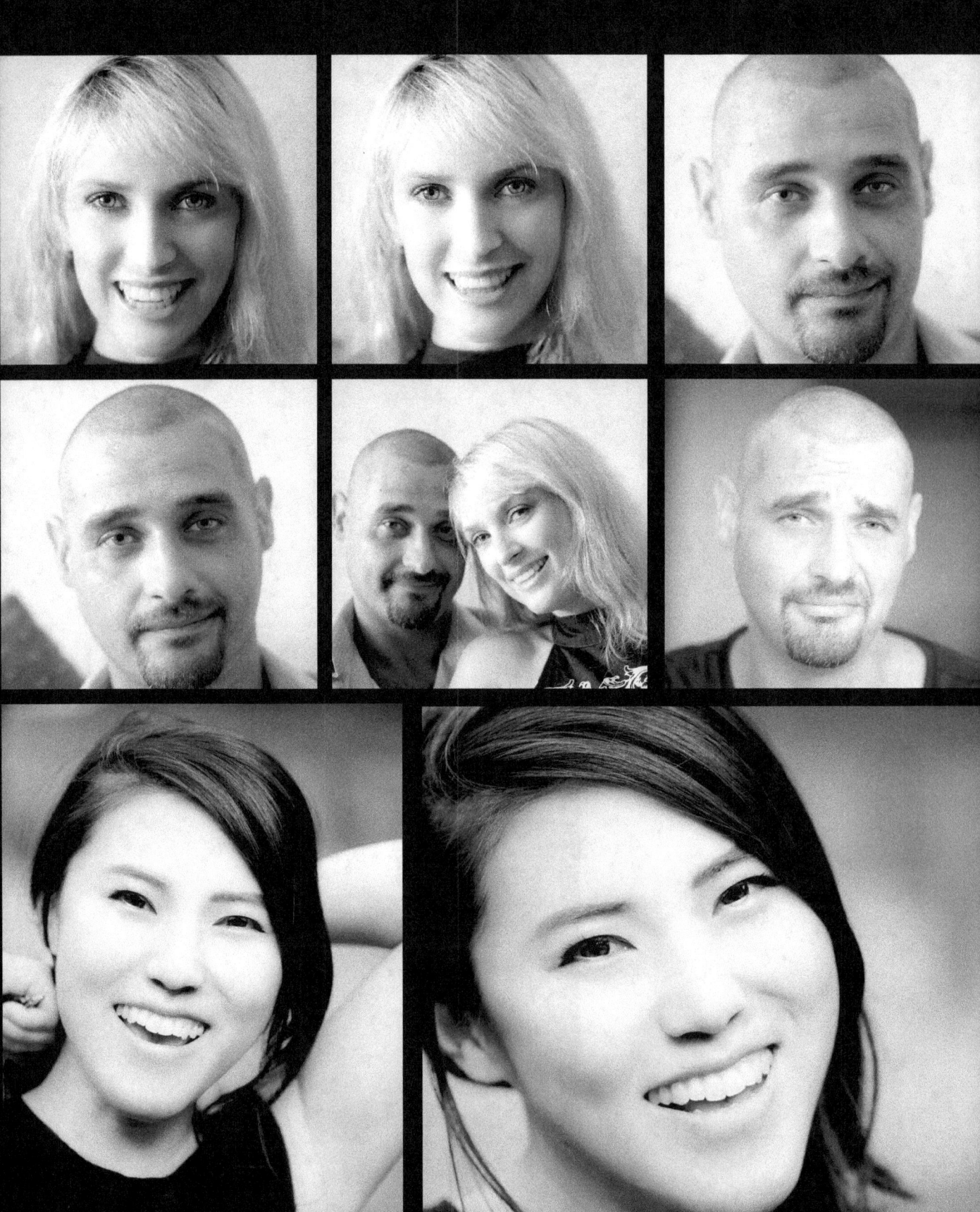

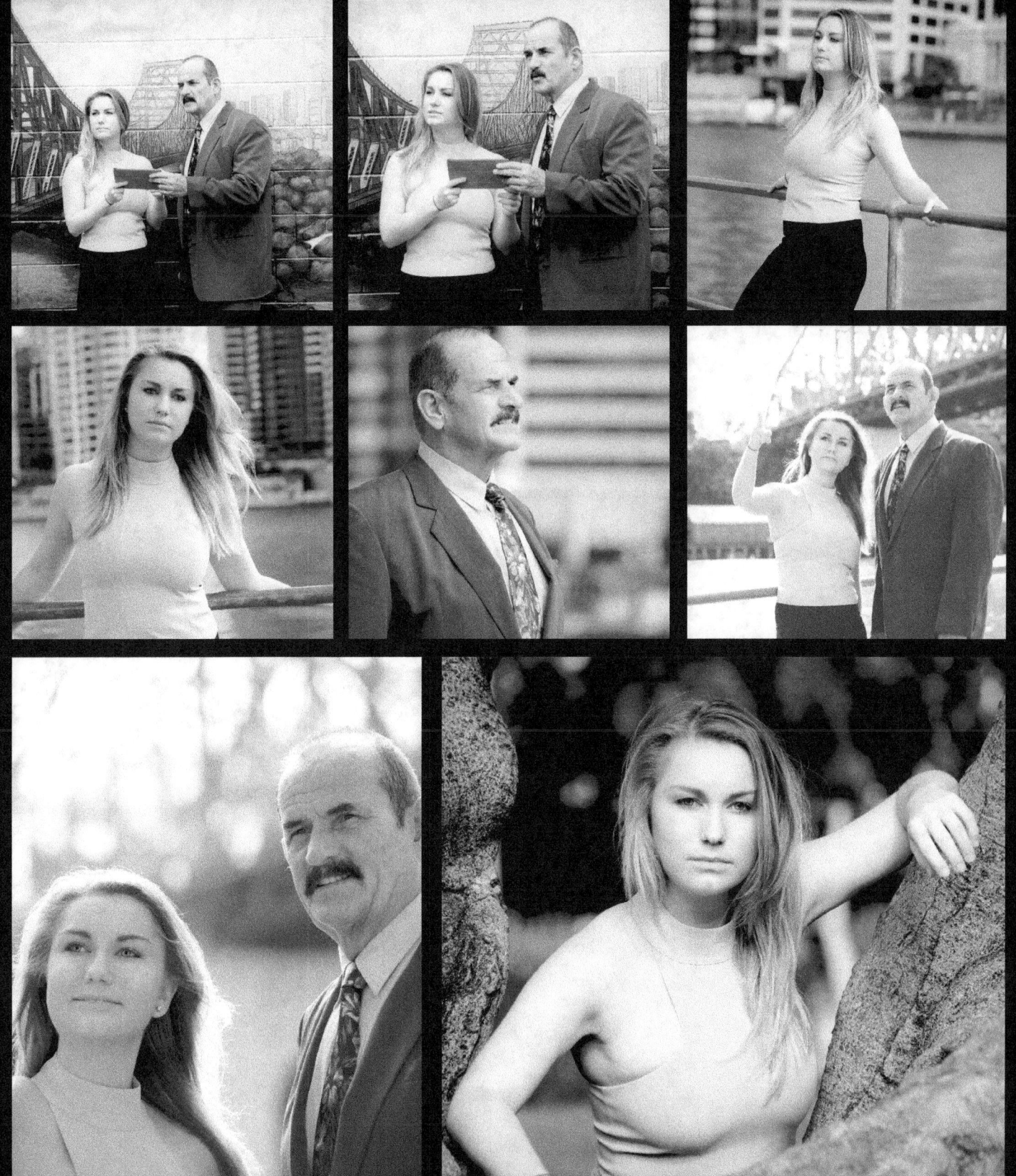

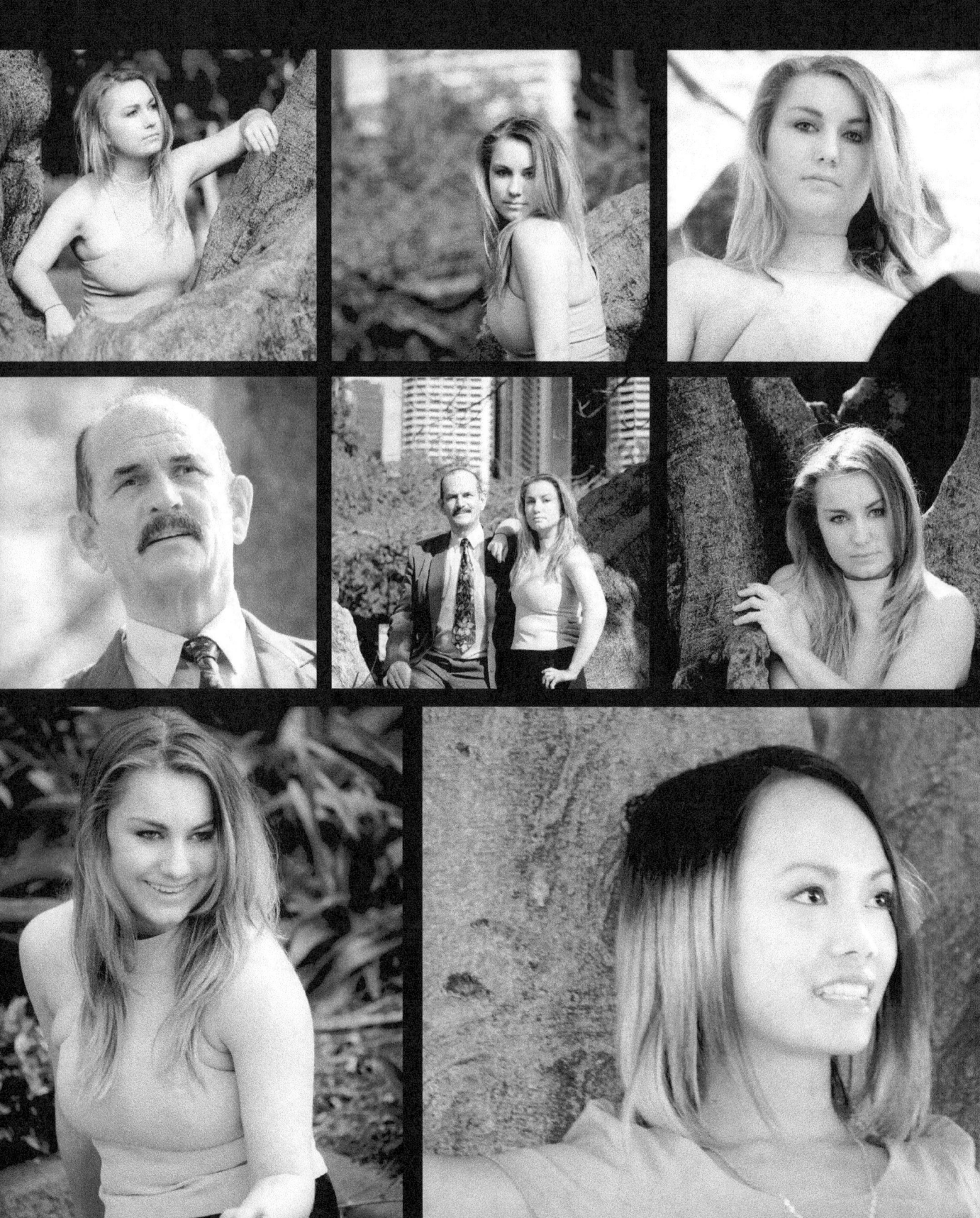

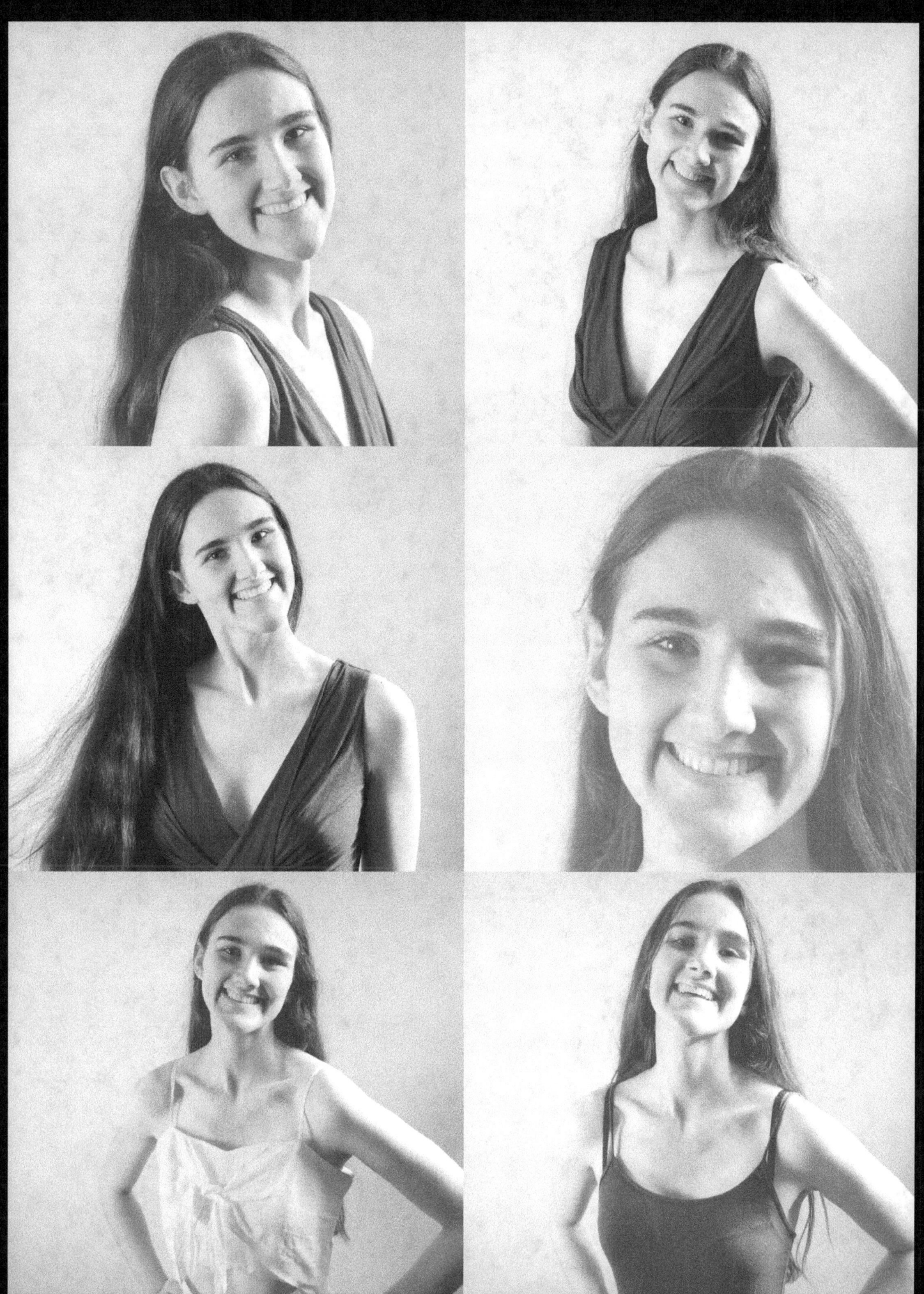

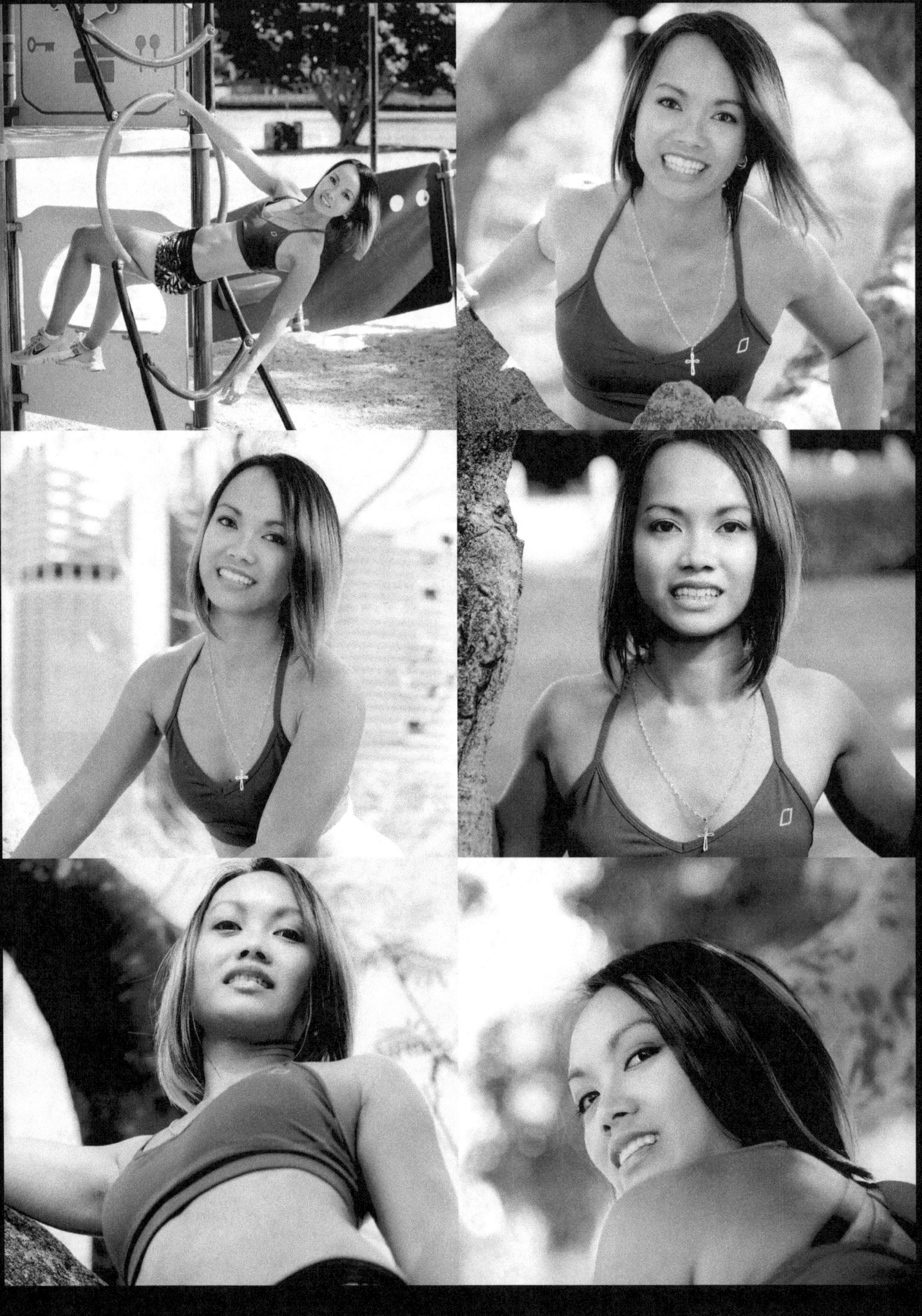

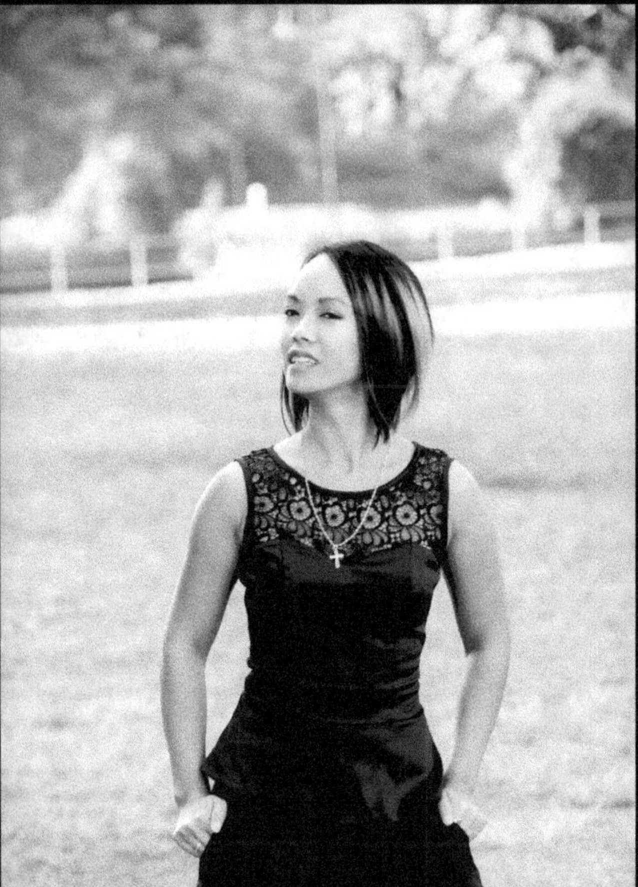

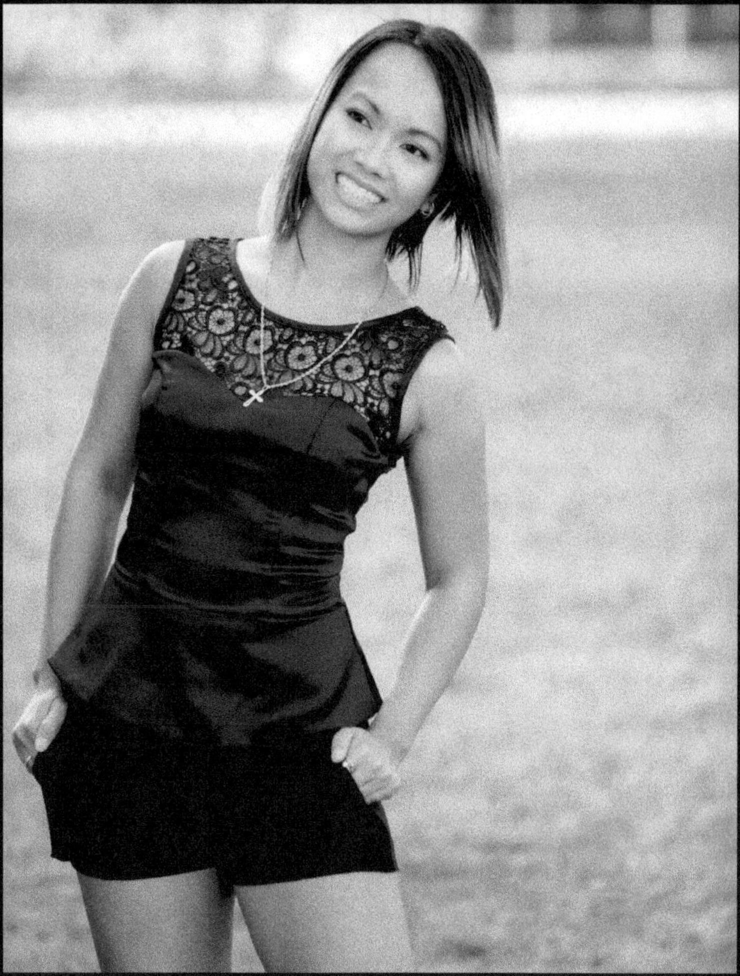

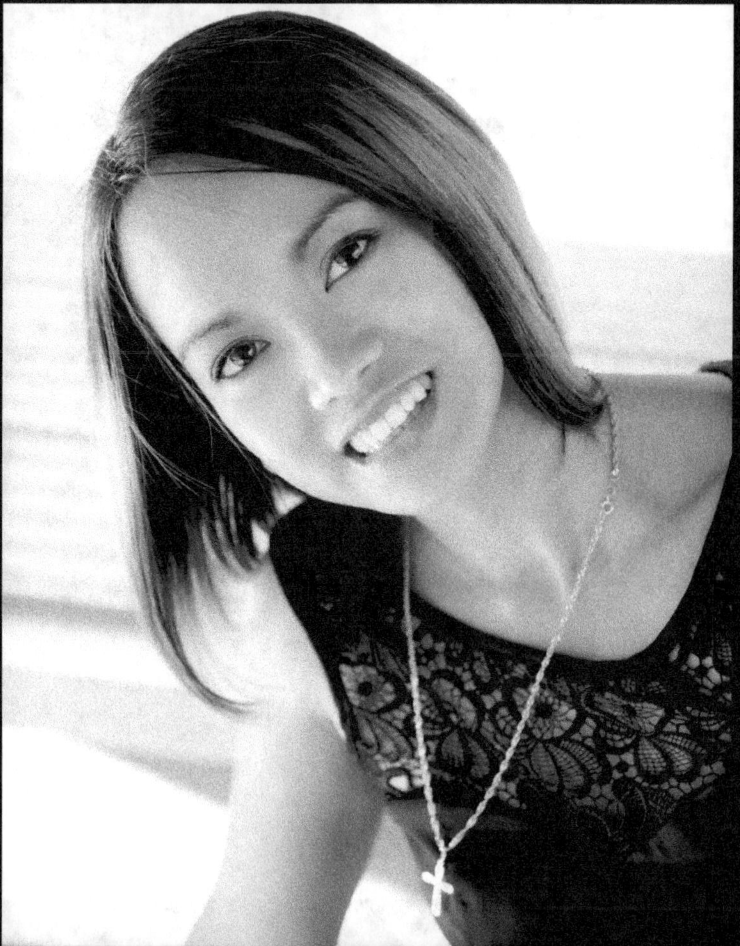

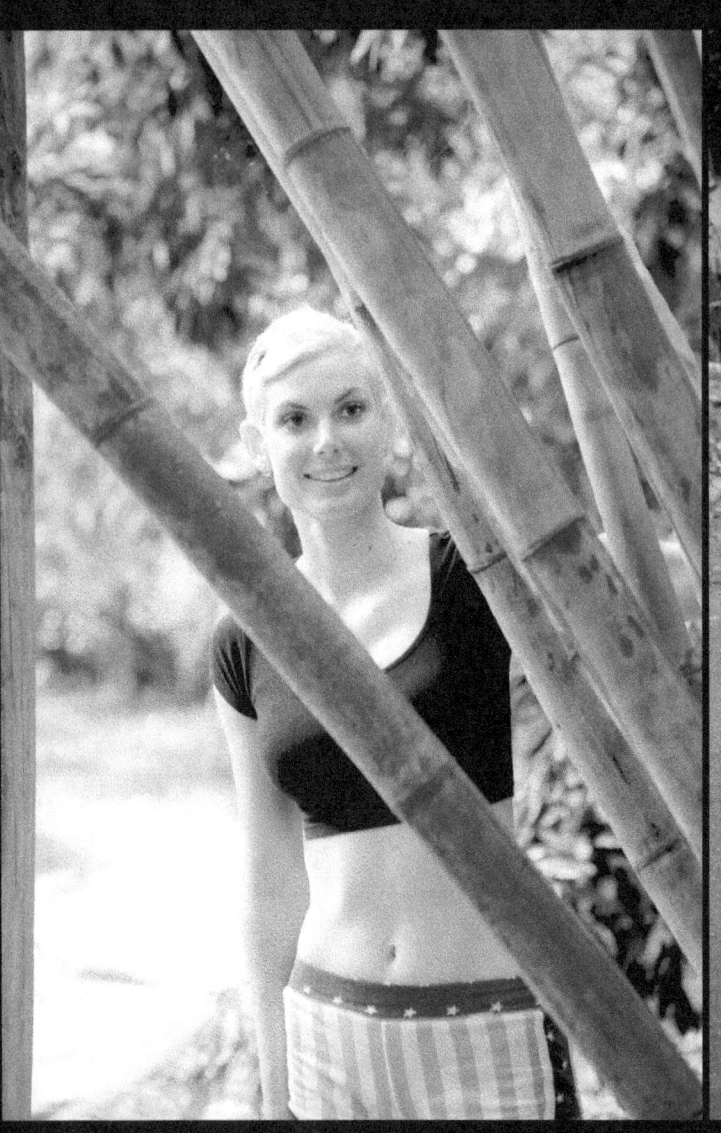
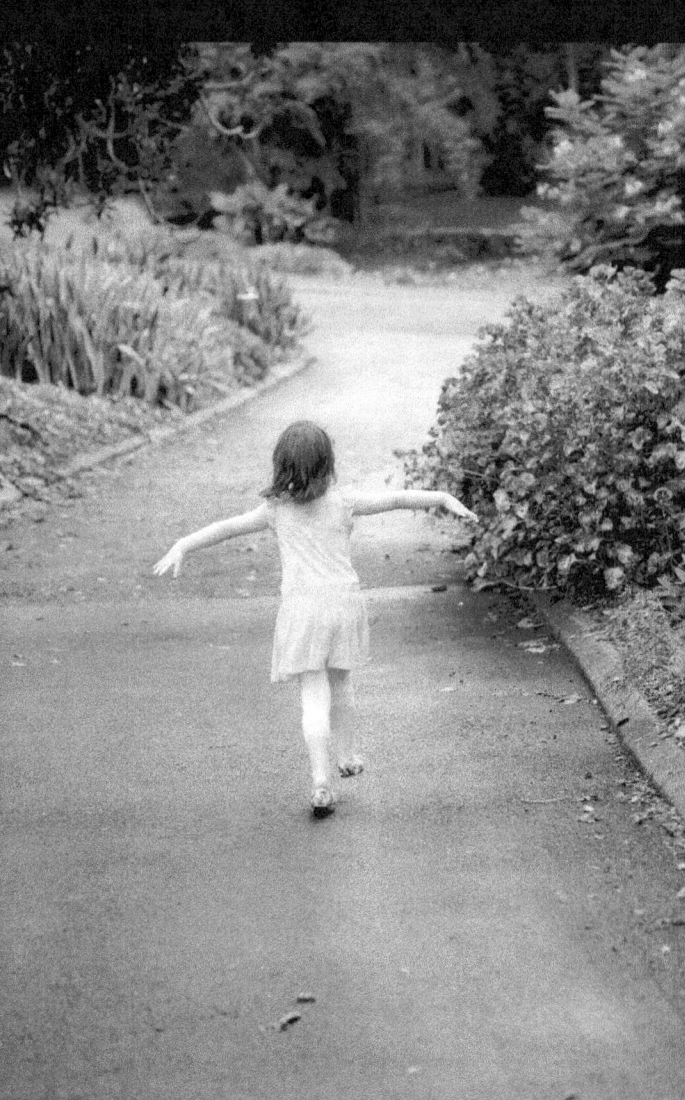
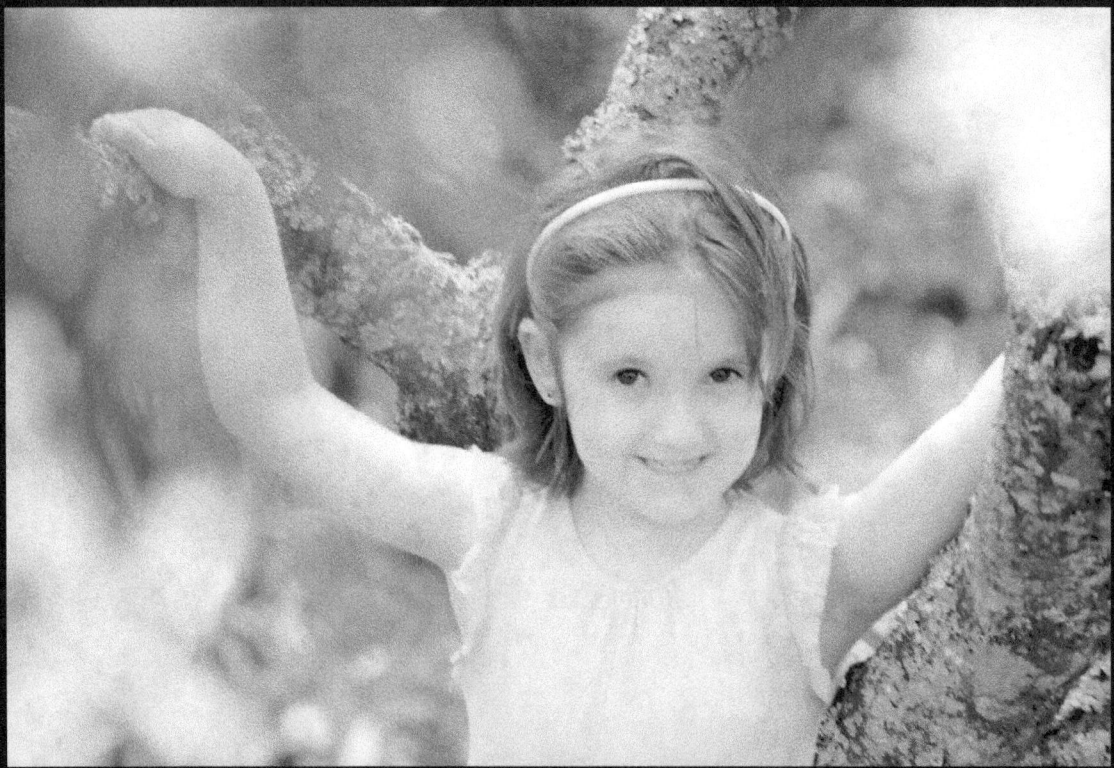

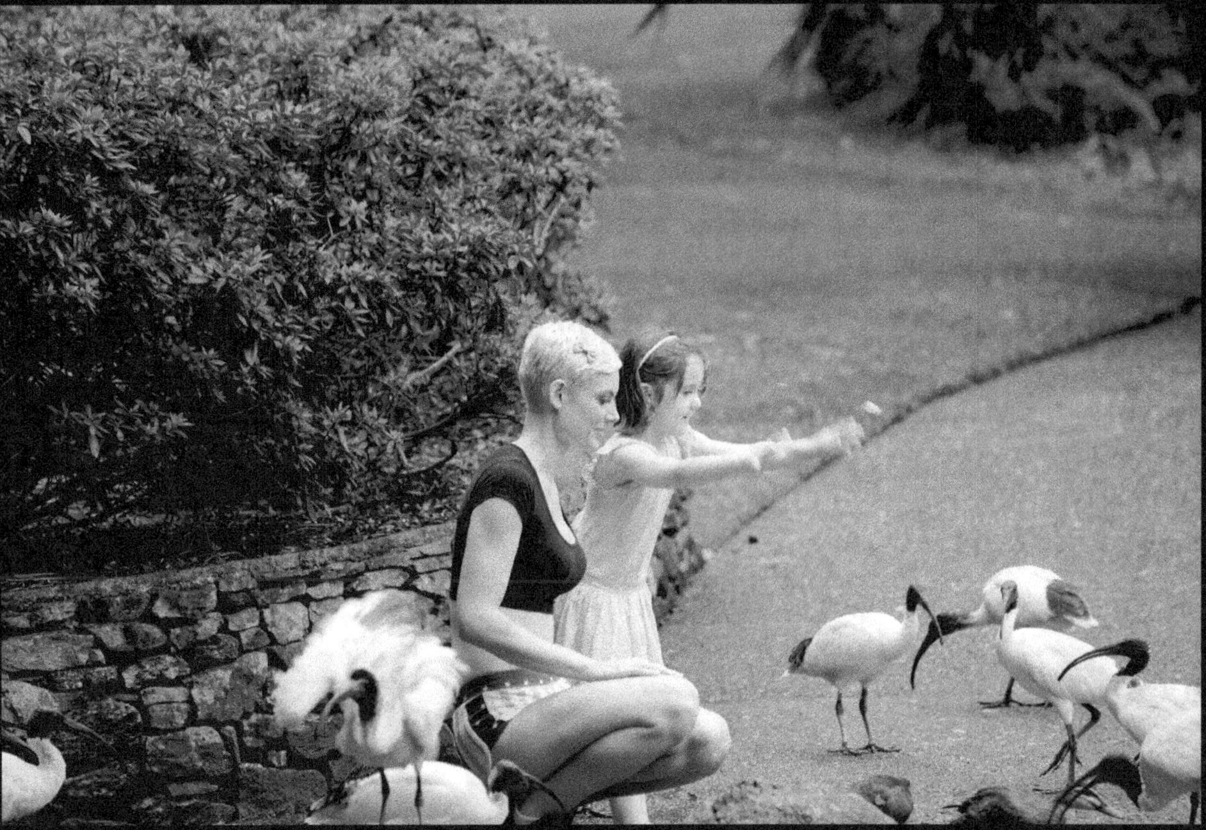

My Coot-tha Botanic Gardens pages 50 and 51

page 51

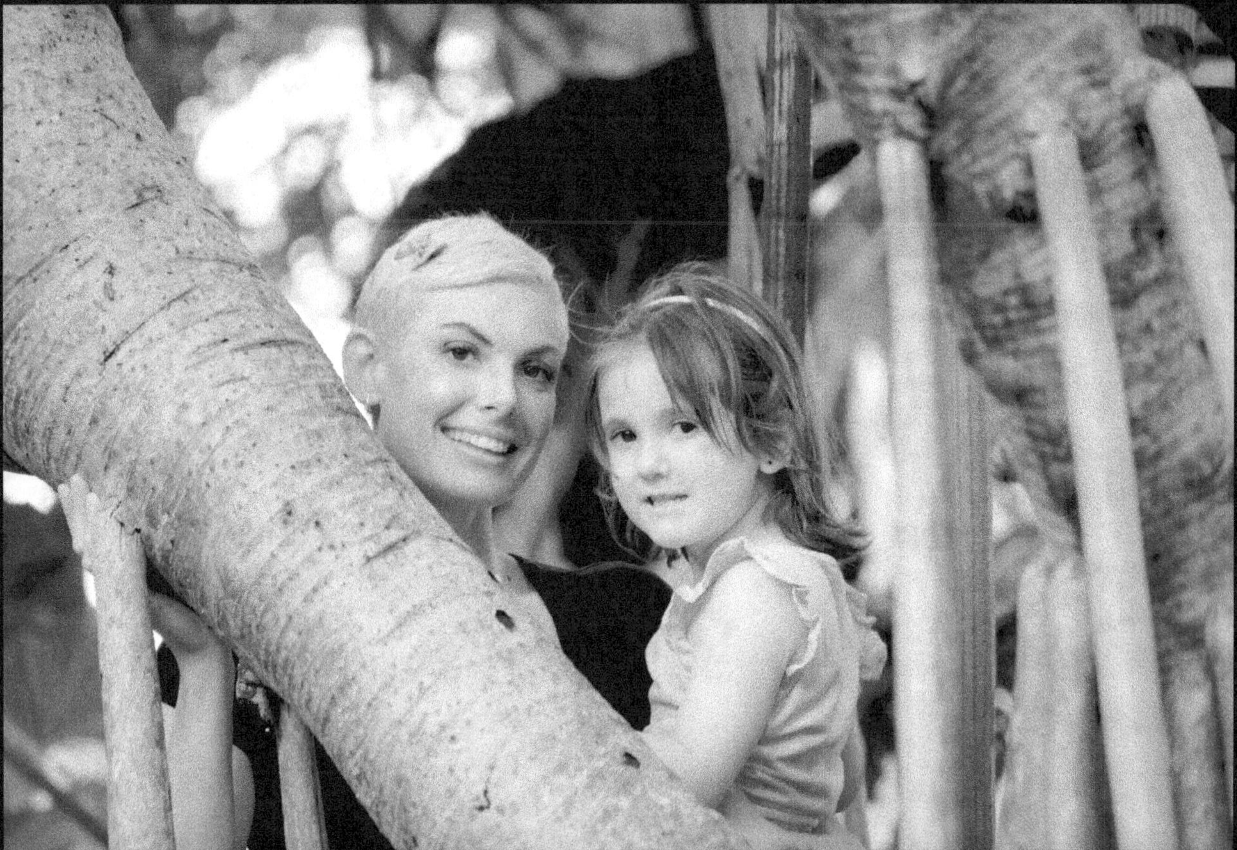

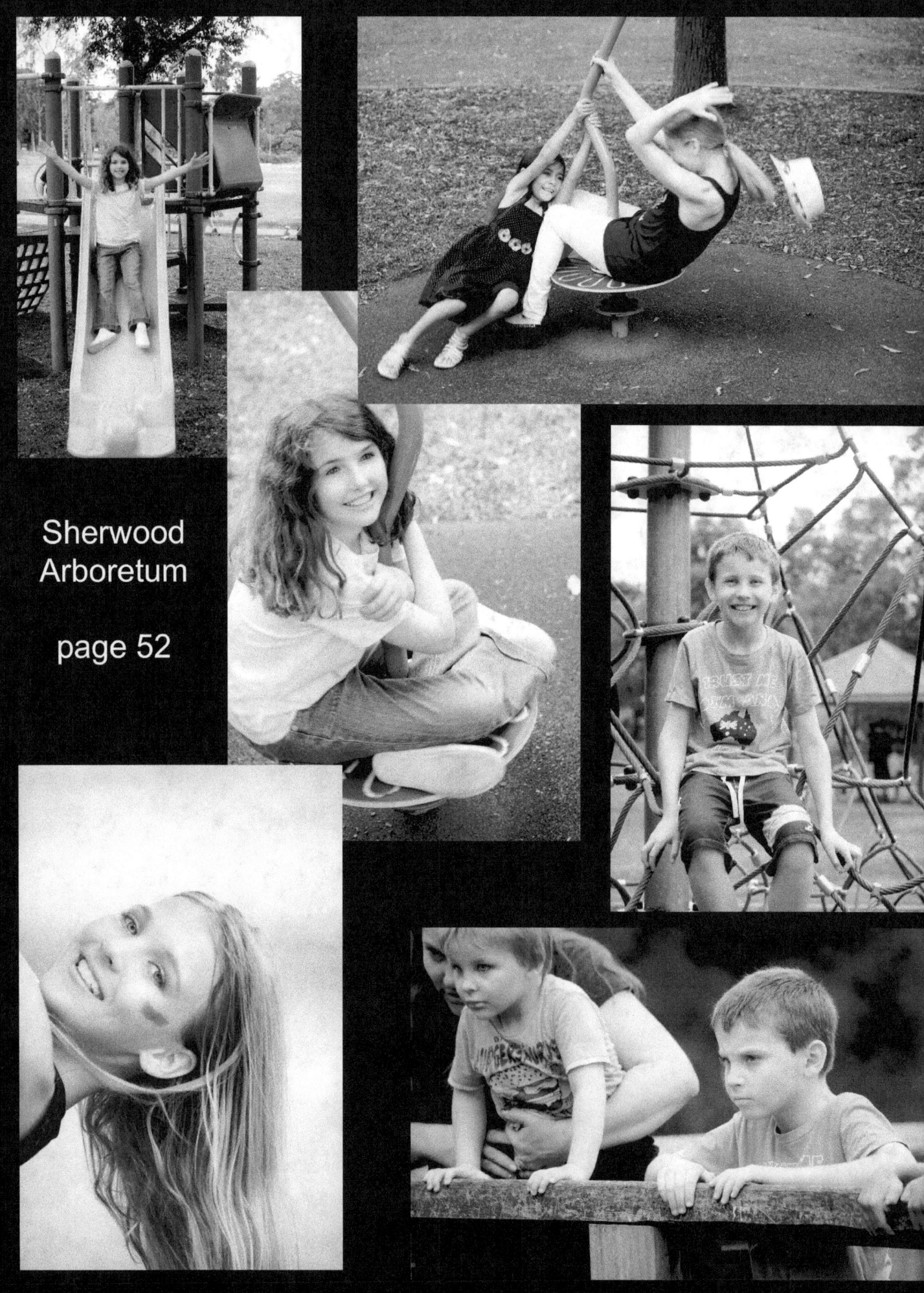

Sherwood
Arboretum

page 52